NEW SCHOOLS FOR A NEW AGE

GOODYEAR EDUCATION SERIES

Theodore W. Hipple, Editor
University of South Carolina at
Spartanburg

CHANGE FOR CHILDREN
Sandra N. Kaplan, Jo Ann B. Kaplan,
Sheila K. Madsen, Bette K. Taylor

CREATING A LEARNING ENVIRONMENT
Ethel Breyfogle, Pamela Santich, Ronald
Kremer, Susan Nelson, Carol Pitts

DO YOU READ ME?
Arnold Griese

IMAGINE THAT!
Joyce King and Carol Katzman

THE LANGUAGE ARTS IDEA BOOK
Joanne D. Schaff

THE LEARNING CENTER BOOK
Tom Davidson, Phyllis Fountain, Rachel
Grogan, Verl Short, Judy Steely, Katherine
Freeman

LOVING AND BEYOND
Joe Abruscato and Jack Hassard

MAINSTREAMING LANGUAGE ARTS
AND SOCIAL STUDIES
Charles R. Coble, Anne Adams, Paul B.
Hounshell

MAINSTREAMING SCIENCE AND MATH
Charles R. Coble, Anne Adams, Paul B.
Hounshell

NEW SCHOOLS FOR A NEW AGE
William Georgiades, Reuben Hilde, Grant
Macaulay

ONE AT A TIME ALL AT ONCE
Jack E. Blackburn and Conrad Powell

THE OTHER SIDE OF THE REPORT
CARD
Larry Chase

AN OUNCE OF PREVENTION PLUS A
POUND OF CURE
Ronald W. Bruton

REACHING TEENAGERS
Don Beach

THE READING CORNER
Harry W. Forgan

A SURVIVAL KIT FOR TEACHERS AND
PARENTS
Myrtle T. Collins and DWane R. Collins

THE WHOLE COSMOS CATALOG OF
SCIENCE ACTIVITIES
Joe Abruscato and Jack Hassard

WILL THE REAL TEACHER PLEASE
STAND UP? 2nd edition
Mary C. Greer and Bonnie Rubinstein

A YOUNG CHILD EXPERIENCES
Sandra N. Kaplan, Jo Ann B. Kaplan,
Sheila K. Madsen, Bette K. Gould

NEW SCHOOLS FOR A NEW AGE

William Georgiades
Chairman of the Dept. of Curriculum and Instruction
School of Education
University of Southern California

Reuben Hilde
Associate Adjunct Professor
Loma Linda University

Grant Macaulay
Associate Adjunct Professor
Loma Linda University

Goodyear Publishing Company, Inc.
Santa Monica, California 90401

Library of Congress Cataloging in
Publication Data

Georgiades, William.
New schools for a new age.

(Goodyear education series)
Bibliography: p. 189
Includes index.
1. Individualized instruction. 2.
Education — United States — 1965- I.
Hilde, Reuben, joint author. II. Macaulay,
Grant, joint author. III. Title.
LB1031.G47   371.39'4   76-9909
ISBN 0-87620-622-4

Y-6224-3

Current Printing (last digit):
10 9 8 7 6 5 4 3 2 1

Printed in the United States of America

Production Editor: Janice Gallagher
Copy Editor: Jackie Estrada

Text and Cover Design: Karol Holden

Illustrations: Howard Saunders

To those who wonder what's wrong with education,
To those who dream of something better,
And to the educators who strive to make the dream come true,
This book is dedicated.

CONTENTS

PREFACE

In a world in which political and religious institutions are in constant flux, it is only reasonable that education and schooling should also be fluid. In recent years, we have seen emerge a wide range of innovative efforts in education, efforts designed to improve the quality of schooling for all American young people. Among the most significant recent efforts has been "the individualization of instruction" with "continuous progress education" as its core.

Attempts to develop instructional systems designed to meet the needs of the individual have appeared and disappeared throughout the history of American education. Although we have not yet developed the means to implement genuinely individualized education for everyone, we have increasingly identified a wide range of options and directions.

This book is devoted to a discussion of such options. We have attempted to cope, in a palatable and digestible way, with the question of education for the individual, rather than education for the masses. In a democracy, such as that found in the United States, individualized education is consistent with the values of the society. To deny systems of schooling designed for the individual is to deny some of the basic tenets of a democratic society.

The authors are well aware of the fact that it is much easier to change vocabulary than to change practice. Too frequently, new models for learning, such as team teaching, nongraded programs, curriculum packaging, and flexible scheduling, are merely attempts to avoid the reality of a genuinely individualized instructional system. Ofttimes, these and other efforts have become ends in and of themselves, resulting in little or no progress.

We hope that this book will make the concept of individualized education more meaningful and more realistic to parents, students, and educators. There is no simplistic, one-step way to change schools to cater to the needs of the individual. The development of genuinely individualized instructional systems demands continuing commitment. In addition, such programs demand a realistic understanding of the process of individualized instruction. This book is designed to provide some of the clues in implementing such a process. It is an attempt to communicate emerging directions, as well as a sense of movement, a sense of purpose, and an increasing sense of "know-how." The authors hope that it will enable committed practitioners to find more effective ways to individualize learning environments for all persons.

Individualized instruction is more than a contemporary educational mania. It is more than a passion for quick innovation and change. It is a commitment to the very ideals of a democratic society. This commitment can be seen in the underlying assumptions of individualized instruction:

1. School systems that penalize persons because they cannot progress at the same rate as others are discriminatory.
2. Schools that penalize students with different kinds of cultural beginnings by lock stepping them into the concept of credit equals time are antihumane.
3. These systems must give way to programs of learning and education that allow individuals to grow at rates commensurate with both interests and abilities.

Beyond the clatter of "deschooling," we will undoubtedly see substantial changes in the organization of systems for learning. We will see the increased adaptation of practices that base credit upon performance, not upon time. We will see increasing application of the process of diagnosis, prescription, and evaluation, rather than starting all students at the same point, exposing all to the same experience, and expecting equal achievement at the same point in time.

The authors of this book are of the conviction that gradually but surely, and with determination, school systems will move toward programs of education that recognize persons as individuals. The miracle of individualized education will not occur tomorrow, but through hard work and diligent application it will emerge in the decades ahead.

PART ONE

THE CONCEPT

We must accept the students
where they are and help them move up the
ladder at their own rate—keeping
them functioning at the optimum level
of their abilities.

A FIRE AND ITS AFTERGLOW

The sound of crashing glass shatters the stillness of the night. Sirens shriek as large red trucks with their ladders and clinging firemen rumble through the darkened streets. Day dawns. Broken glass crunches under the weight of inspecting footsteps. The gathering crowd is met with the depressing smell of fire-charred wood and wet broken plaster. The remaining walls of the school building are decorated with grotesque, spray-painted swastikas and four-letter words; misspelled messages tell the authorities where to go and what to do. Shaggy, unkempt weirdos—always instant suspects—linger on the fringes. Youthful occupants of an overloaded car needle the spectators with catcalls and obscene jokes.

REPORTS AND OPINIONS

As the television newscaster describes another of the recurring scenes of school vandalism, Joe Sixpack, Helen Housewife, and thousands of other not-so-silent Americans editorialize on their own:

"What's this generation coming to?"

"When I was a kid, we either went to school and behaved ourselves, or we quit and went to work."

"When these kids are told to jump, the only question they should ask is, 'How high?' "

"Believe me, if I was one of those authorities, every one of those punks would be behind bars!"

"They ought to draft every one of them."

"Yeah, Joe, but even the army has gone soft—with all that long hair. And Uncle Sam is on his knees now with that stuff about 'The army wants to join you!' Can you imagine?"

So Joe Sixpack sits back and reminisces about the good old days of "Old Blood and Guts," the tough leader with the pearl handles at his side and his whip in hand. Meanwhile, his children, Dick and Jane (you've heard of them) slip out into the evening, equipped with symbols of their own way of life. Decked in unisex clothes and armed with their own language (both verbal and nonverbal), they move in a paradoxical world of ear-shattering music that contrasts strikingly with their own gentle manners. Every mannerism, every antiwar declaration, and each new friend brought home adds to old Joe Sixpack's ulcer problem. In disgust he turns again to the refrigerator . . .

On a more sophisticated level, the response to the televised report on school vandalism takes a different tack. Combining a pinch of truth with a fistful of egotism, the naive realist suggests other remedies for the problems facing American education. The tough-minded insist on a get-tough policy in intellectual matters: Concentrate on developing the intellect; set up programs similar to European education (whatever that is); and see to it that the intellectual resources of our youth are directed to the task of national survival. After all, what we're facing is a matter of national and international catastrophe and annihilation!

The politically minded turn in the direction of legislation as the primary solution to this vandalism problem and the problem of "wayward youth." Legislation is needed to put teeth into educational standards. Legislation is needed to fund the projects to restore these standards (and to see that all of our kids achieve about the national norms!). Those placing their faith in political action as the medium for solving the problems of education reason that we should get a dollar's worth of education for each dollar invested. Supported by this logic and other obvious "facts," they seek to build into their legislative measures a means of seeing to it that educators (and teachers in particular) face up to their responsibilities. "Accountability" becomes the password—the panacea for solving the delinquency problem, the vandalism, the reading problem, and all the other symptoms that pose as the real problem.

While the politician, in stentorian tones, proclaims Accountability as the key to educational reform, another problem solver enters the scene—the great American businessman. Famed for his basic know-how and his utilitarian bootstrap philosophy, he proposes a solution that fascinates the politicians and catches the ear of Mr. and Mrs. Joe Sixpack. Thus, through convincing and reassuring logic, the American businessman, who has perfected his line into a dollar-making science, sells the "voucher system" to the waiting educational world. The overburdened taxpayer is intrigued by another proposal.

"So your kid can't read! Well, we have a plan for which you pay us **x** dollars, and we will raise your son's reading ability from level two to level five. We'll do this in six months' time; and if we don't get him to that level, you get your money back."

With a little bit of Las Vegas in them, and a lot of faith in the dollar-for-dollar philosophy, Joe Sixpack and his wife, prodded by the problem-solving politician, decide: "Yeah, I think I'll buy that!"

ENTER, THE EDUCATOR

On the periphery (and that's where cautious educators generally are), the reflective educator contemplates the dilemma. Clad in tweed suit and vest, with pipe held at a jaunty angle and match poised to strike, with beard and hair longer than in past years and eyes narrowed to a squint, this impressive pedagogue mulls over the answers proposed by political leaders and supported by the confident, ever-pressing businessman. The professor is not so sure (and that's the scholarly position to take) that these ready answers, these legislative acts and business ventures, will really get to the heart of the matter. After all, teaching is an art. We're dealing with kids, not with the mass production of automobiles. The professor is somewhat afraid of the computer punch card, and he turns to a major consideration—the "humane" aspect of education. He feels that he must look upon the students in our educational system as individual human beings, each distinct and unique.

As this reflective educator muses further, he finds that other basic considerations emerge. From these considerations he, and others like him, produce a series of innovative approaches. These approaches range from certain philosophical concepts, which may be highly theoretical, to the very practical curriculum procedures that the professor and his colleagues help to establish in the local schools.

Even for the professor, the road to educational change and curriculum improvement is not smooth. As much as he would like to introduce those elements that would bring about a solution to the problems of delinquency and vandalism, he finds that ready answers are just not there. In the first place, the solutions seem so complex. The problems involved go deeper than he is able to probe—so he spends much time in theorizing. He writes and speaks of the social issues, the psychological hangups, the political differences and the philosophical values that vary with the numerous views of education taken by leading educators.

And the more the professor theorizes, the further he gets from a large segment of those educators on the front lines of education—the teachers and local administrators. They, in turn, react to the professor's concepts as ivory-towered, theoretical, and impractical.

"What he needs," they solemnly declare, "is to spend some time every year teaching. Then what would he do with those high-sounding theories?"

BANDWAGONITIS

Not all of the front liners react negatively to the proposed educational innovations. Some possess a fever that might be called "bandwagonitis." They jump on every innovation that parades by the educational viewing stand. These enthusiasts proclaim with almost evangelistic zeal the good that is developing as a result of their new program at School Z.

With the freedom of a politician we change our metaphor in the middle of a point—and we adopt a more earthy illustration: Thus, on the fertile soil of the field of education, school plants begin to grow from seed ideas germinated in some university hothouse. Innovations of all kinds are developed. Generally, these efforts are praised most by those who nurture them—by those who have planted the seed. The thoughtful critic views these praises as somewhat flowery and artificial. This same critic not only demands a more scientific evaluation but expects to see an appropriate harvest. (Meanwhile, jokesters cannot resist the temptation to refer to budding geniuses of education who turned out to be blooming idiots.) Nevertheless, in an effort to keep in the forefront of educational matters and to keep from being surpassed by neighboring schools or districts, individual educational leaders promote an innovation or two that they attempt to graft onto the school plant. Testimonies to such endeavors are myriad:

"We have adopted an ongoing program of flexible scheduling at our school, and it's really working well. The teachers are happy with it, and the students think it is great!"

"You should stop by to see our team teaching program. We've divided our classes into large groups, small groups, and independent study time. The teachers feel that it is working well. We're having a little trouble with the students during independent study time, but they seem to be happier than they were under the old program."

These brief testimonies typify the extent to which most innovations are evaluated. Scientific, thorough evidence as to the effectiveness of these educational ventures is generally missing.

Reports multiply. Countless books, journals, magazines, and newspapers extol the unique efforts of enthusiastic innovators. Team teaching, vouchers, nongrading, accountability, open classrooms, individualized instruction, contracts, LAPs (Learning Activities Packages), modular scheduling, and numerous other innovative thrusts parade across the pages of the literature. Educators would hide their heads if they were to be exposed as unacquainted with the latest innovations.

In this effort to be up-to-date on happenings in education, educators adopt an innovation so that they might be able to assert that "big things are going on at our school." In this insecure endeavor to be recognized as problem-solving educators, they build a series of fronts or facades around themselves. But all too often, behind the veneer, the same old practices are carried on. Teachers lose respect for the innovative enthusiasts; students fail to recognize any sense of direction to the program (and cleverly manage to go their own way); and parents long for the good old days, the one-room school, and the return of the three R's.

MEANWHILE THE YOUTH

Meanwhile, the delinquent youth, the arsonist, the child who moves along the fringes of society, is no respecter of programs. School buildings continue to burn whether they serve as the site for special programs or whether they are the setting for the most tradition-bound academic programs—the torch is lit, the paint is splattered, the vilifications are spewed.

So the search goes on. Some seek out the guilty youth. Others search for the meaningful education that will solve the problems that not only continue to exist but are ever expanding, growing more acute and costly.

Not all innovators are to be accused of putting up an educational front. Many are seriously searching for the answers to the difficult and complex problems of education and society. Many are deeply hurt by the incisive criticism of experts from other fields. And certainly, many of the innovations introduced do constitute an improvement over past procedures, even if this advance may be measured only in improved attitudes and improved morale.

UNANSWERED QUESTIONS

Serious questions still need to be asked. Why should we bring in a flexible schedule? What is to be accomplished through team teaching? Is the voucher system the answer to the basic problems of education? Examine any new proposal for educational improvement (certainly most of those cited have been around for some time); does it direct its attention to solving the basic problems?

By the way, what are the basic problems? Is vandalism the real problem? Is it the dropout? Is the ever-rising cost of education the real issue? (Perhaps we should inquire into the costs of not educating our youth.)

Are we to revive the ideals of patriotism and educate youth to be the instrument for our national survival? (What an inhuman thought—producing atomic age cannon fodder!)

And dare we reintroduce the integration issue? Will successful integration bring about the solution to our dilemma? Is there a mastermind on the horizon who will bring about a satisfactory solution to the busing problem?

Can it be that our proposals for solving educational problems are actually polarizing us even more? Are we further from agreement since these proposals have been introduced?

Are the questions we ask and the solutions we propose bringing us closer together? Are they bringing us nearer to the solutions we really want? Have we identified the basic problems in order that the real solutions may be found? Many educators have not hesitated to suggest solutions.

PROPHETS AMONG US

Periodically, writers of great stature lead us to reexamine the issues of education. They question the direction in which educational leaders are moving. These critics seem to have their intellectual fingers on the pulse of American feelings and world concern. The reader may recall, for example, that in the era of progressive education one man who had such a sense of timing was Charles Allen Prosser. He succeeded in introducing resolutions that identified society's concern for the slower 50 percent of students who were not college bound.

Much later, with World War II out of the way, the heat of a new cold war was on. Then came the American humiliation of the Russian Sputnik orbiting the earth. With the timing of an ancient seer, the outspoken Admiral Rickover, the distinguished developer of the atomic submarine, began to attack the American school system. Needless to say, when such a distinguished critic labeled the American school system a national failure, the schools—and the educators in particular—were shaken to their foundations. Educators, formerly viewed as pillars, quaked as Congress shook up the educational scene through its investigating committees.

A calmer critic, highly respected for his educational and scientific accomplishments, James B. Conant, introduced a more careful analysis of American education. He made an extensive study of the American high school, concluding that the school systems were better than they may have been credited by critics; but he made a number of recommendations for improvement. These recommendations included a new emphasis on the academic development of gifted and bright young people.

It became stylish among educators to compare their programs with the Conant recommendations. Even though there were educators who were not in full accord with the Conant concepts, seldom did they take a position in opposition to the views of this distinguished scholar.

During the years that followed, it appears that educators began to develop a more secure attitude toward the criticisms that were fired at them. Nevertheless, educators could no longer rest on the traditions of the past. They had to investigate, try, innovate if they were to be among those alert to the relevant issues. Typical educators were too ready to latch on to curriculum plans, scheduling schemes, and any ideas that might put them and their schools on the map. As a result, numerous designs and plans were launched, floated, but finally sank into educational oblivion. Writers divided into conflicting camps. The literature described, testified, and recommended; it extolled, praised, and made unverified claims. But it also advocated caution; it criticized and clamored against the questionable practices that masqueraded as innovations.

In recent years several serious, discerning writers have been candidates for the title of newest of the prophets. With discriminating skill, they have isolated factors that must be carefully considered if we are to meet today's challenges in education. One of the foremost of these analysts is the highly respected Charles E. Silberman. In his stimulating work, **Crisis in the Classroom,** Silberman demonstrates his insightfulness. If the Rickovers and Conants attracted such universal attention in the recent past, Silberman's work deserves equal attention.

Silberman makes no attempt to discredit the large number of innovative endeavors now under way in education. In fact, he is supportive of these efforts. He does, however, touch a very tender spot on the body of academia. He expresses it in one shattering word—"mindlessness." Many splendid things are going on. Educators are trying potentially effective theories; funds are being allocated; humans are becoming humane, showing concern for the individual; instructional technology is being perfected and implemented; sound learning theories are being taught; curriculum development is gaining more serious attention; evaluation systems are being reevaluated; flexibility in scheduling is being promoted; effective utilization of professional and paraprofessional staff members is being studied. And yet, through all these worthwhile thrusts (in the words of Nathan Pusey in **The Age of the Scholar**), there is the "haunting feeling that all is not well."

It becomes difficult to avoid Silberman's conclusion—mindlessness! Efforts are not coordinated, not directed toward the solution of an underlying problem that is endemic to all education. In other words, we are coming up with solutions but we don't know the problem we are trying to solve. We are almost schizophrenic in our search for answers, but first we need to identify the basic problem. Writers have given much thought to this agonizing question. Meanwhile, Silberman's "mindlessness" has taken on the proportions of a large neon sign—flashing on and off during the night of our search. More important than all these considerations—these proposals for educational relevance, reformation, redirection, or whatever—is the identifying of the fundamental problem.

Certainly the basic problem is not vandalism. It cannot be the youth of our day. It is not merely the antiestablishment attitude of a growing number of young people. Even the deep considerations of integration, with its busing problems, cannot be pinned down as the number-one problem. Lack of money, whether due to resistance on the part of taxpayers or to unavailability of federal funds, cannot be labelled as the number-one problem. The passing of further legislation would not be the means of uncovering the basic issue.

AN IDEA

It would be presumptuous for the writers to claim that they have the answer and that all the world has to do is listen. The fact is that educators have for years been treading around in a curricular desert but never far from a refreshing oasis. Some have already been refreshed and have urged others to make a pilgrimage to this oasis.

The concept to which we refer is so startlingly simple in its philosophy that we are amazed that more consideration has not been given to it. It is difficult to believe that we've tramped around in the desert for so long without heading straight for this answer. It is possible that since the principle is so simple, educators may have assumed that any deviation from it could hardly be a cause for serious difficulties. And yet we feel that that is just the case. We hold that variance from this fundamental concept is the greatest cause for the problems that exist in education; whether the educator overlooks, ignores, or rejects this principle, the results may be the same—trouble (with students, parents, taxpayers, teachers, society in general, and the demands of the times).

The principle: A meaningful education requires that we accept the student where he is (intellectually, socially, emotionally, physically) and help him to move up the ladder at his own rate—keeping him functioning at the optimum level of his abilities. It means providing an atmosphere of acceptance and establishing a climate in which the student can gain success through a reasonable amount of effort. It is an education in which the teacher provides learning opportunities that meet the needs and interests of each child, while helping the child gain a sense of direction. It is an education that evaluates the child's accomplishments as they relate to his personal potential. It is an education that places the teacher side-by-side with the student as the two work together for the successful growth of the learner.

In three words, it may be called "continuous progress education." A new idea? No. A concept in general practice today? No. A concept with any possibilities for the future. Definitely.

So, what's new? If educators have alluded to it, if some pioneers have adopted it, if there are countless articles relating to it, why make so much of it now? It needs to be examined because (in most cases) it has only been put into practice on a superficial or fragmented basis. (In Chapter 3 we will deal briefly with its history and with evidences of its use.) We have as our objective a four-fold task:

First, we will identify the concept of continuous progress in its ideal form. Unless certain encrusted misconceptions are removed, it will provide no more of the answers than many other concepts.

Second, we will identify the factors basic to the successful implementation of continuous progress education. This will be the thrust of Part II of the book.

Third, we will set forth certain models, packages, or outlines depicting the way in which continuous progress might be implemented. This will be the task of Part III.

Finally, we will attempt to ward off the wolves. We will examine the views of the critics.

Few would compare traditional education with the modern automobile, but the parallel is not too remote.

The numerous innovations tacked on to the old educational system merely decorate the exterior but do not get rid of the basic problems.

SERIOUS QUESTIONS CONCERNING THE STATUS QUO

2

Having been blitzkrieged by so many solutions to society's problems, the reader may be tempted to ask, "What's wrong with the status quo? Why can't we just shore up our traditional programs? What's wrong with just doing a better job at what we have been doing? Look at the great leaders this country has developed. Aren't they the products of our society and its school system?"

UNSATISFACTORY ALTERNATIVES

Recently one of the authors of this book saw the answers to these questions graphically illustrated. A young student teacher was putting his physical education classes through the paces in certain track and field events. He had successive squads take their turns running the 440-yard dash. In one group, a young boy, apparently the victim of polio, ran courageously around the track. When he faced the strong head wind down the home stretch, it was too much for him. He faded, slowed down, and dropped to the ground alongside the track. The student coach called out to him to get up and keep moving so he wouldn't get cramps. Then the young teacher came up, put his arm on the boy's shoulder, and gave him words of encouragement.

Suppose that the requirements for a passing grade in that class included running the 440 in 70 seconds, and that if a student wasn't able to accomplish this he would have to repeat the course the following year. Here it is hoped that he would have improved enough so that he could become capable of passing the test. But note, this approach doesn't help the student and likely will not motivate him to succeed the second time around. In fact, when we face reality (a difficult task in the world of education), we can readily predict that the student will do no better the second time around. Most educators and educational systems have abandoned this first approach.

An alternative approach appears to be much more satisfactory: Adopt a humane attitude and give the student a "social pass" on to the next grade. But suppose this student is given his social pass on to the next physical education class, where the standard for acceptable performance in the 440-yard dash is 65 seconds (an arbitrary figure set by the writer, who would have had difficulty even if the time were doubled). The student who could not meet the 70-second standard is now faced with a more rigorous requirement. It quickly becomes apparent that he will not make it.

In such a setting, the student must adjust to failure. Here he is forced to live in an atmosphere of failure or an even more uncomfortable setting—an atmosphere of pity. To put it bluntly, he is a misfit. He's placed in a setting in which he cannot hope to experience success. The approach that initially appeared to be humane proves to be just the opposite.

We can almost feel the book flying through the air as the irate coach lets go a few unpremeditated expletives. And we wouldn't blame a coach for such a reaction. Few, if any, men or women would be so insensitive to the needs and differences of their students in physical education. And yet, that is exactly what we are doing in the areas of the curriculum carelessly named "academic."

Most educators could cite incidents in which students were asked to perform in areas, or at levels, in which they were almost completely unprepared to function. Researching Shakespeare might be a fascinating activity for a high school student, but it is not a realistic assignment for a student who cannot read. Similarly, algebra might not be the great ogre that it is for so many youth if they were equipped with the basic mathematical tools with which to handle it.

RESPONSES TO FAILURE

The reader might well ask himself, "How would I react if each day of my life I were required to participate in a series of activities in which I faced almost certain failure?" And it's not just a one-shot failure experience. The inappropriately placed student faces an entire series of failures. It is too much to expect to ask him to adjust satisfactorily to such a cruel dilemma.

How does the student react when he faces a succession of continuous failures? Most of us have witnessed a variety of responses. A student may:

1. Assume an outward appearance of carelessness, acting unconcerned over his failures—the class wasn't important anyway.
2. Develop the feeling that the teacher, the school, and even the more able students are against him.
3. Try to compensate for his failures by succeeding in areas outside the school (if he makes this adjustment, he is doing well). In doing so he may adopt a "mature" attitude about the importance of work while discounting the value of formal education.
4. Seethe inside with an increasing hatred toward the society that has placed him in such a humiliating, ego-destroying position. Once in a while this inner volcano erupts in vandalism, fighting, and open defiance of teachers and other authorities.
5. Become very silent in class, never speaking out or responding to learning opportunities or the teacher's questions, drawing within a shell of silence to seek solace and protection from a hostile educational environment.

HOW WE HANDLE THE INCOMPETENTS

Other reactions have been observed, but there is abundant evidence that the present system of education is actually building antisocial, antischool, antiauthority attitudes into a large number of our students.

Generally, society does not treat the misfit with kindness. Witness the baseball fan and his reaction to the inept performance of a ballplayer: "Get the bum out of there! Send him back to Podunk!" It doesn't take much cerebration to realize that the inept ballplayer is very conscious of his errors without being reminded by the vocal fan.

In essence, we have shouted at the unsuccessful student, "Get the bum out of there!" Often the poor student is viewed as a poor citizen. On the surface this may be the case, but it is more likely that the poor student has become a poor citizen because he could not cope with the failures and frustrations into which he has been thrust and held.

STAMPED AND CLASSIFIED

Perhaps the greatest evil emerging from the status quo (here we mean maintaining the traditional approach to education—even with our periodic attempts to improve the graded system) is the strong tendency of educators and parents, and perhaps society at large, to label students. A student's reputation goes before him. If he is thought of as a D student, a slow student, or just plain dumb, this label precedes him to his next class. He is put into a classification from which he rarely escapes. Later in his life, society is often startled and surprised at his success. We well remember a "dumb" kid whose yearly salary before age 30 tripled our salaries (perhaps that tells something else about education—but that consideration does not come under the scope of this present volume). But much more pathetic are the numerous cases in which the labels stuck. Society's evaluations proved accurate—the dumb kid became a bum. Very likely the label had more to do with the kid's failure than did his so-called basic lack of intelligence.

The fact is that our systems of evaluation have been too narrow. They have not been comprehensive enough to enable educators to label students accurately. Yet the present system does label rather permanently, even though that may not be the intent of the wise educator.

SMART KIDS PLAY THE GAME

At the other end of the educational continuum is the smart kid. This straight-A, gifted, bright kid basks in the warmth and comfort of a label that he cherishes. Even through his occasional denials and humble assertions that he is not so smart, his ego is fortified by the reassurances that he's "got it made." In this very different setting, the traditional system is just as faulty as it is in dealing with the "stupid" kid at the other end of the line.

The gifted student often develops another gift—the ability to cool the tests. He becomes test wise; he anticipates the teacher's requirements and succeeds in pulling down an A without even cracking a book. It becomes easy for this student to assume any one of a number of roles. He may play it cool with a sophisticated boredom. In this role, as in other roles, he has an influence on the members of the class. It may, under his leadership, become popular among other students to assume this same casual, complacent attitude toward the class and toward learning in general. And if the teacher concentrates his or her efforts on the average students, the middle group, it gives credence to the gifted student's boredom. The bright student, un-challenged, becomes genuinely bored.

Or, the gifted student may take on the role of super-critic. He challenges the teacher on occasion, showing a depth of knowledge the teacher did not anticipate. The class sees the embarrassment of the teacher; consequently, respect for him and his teaching plum-mets. The threatened teacher becomes almost anti-intellectual in his stance, turning to an indoctrinating approach in which his word is truth and law. He speaks **ex cathedra,** out of the chair of authority, and further alienates himself from the students. This is one of the many ways in which students and teachers end up in juxtaposition—in a stance of encounter: student versus teacher. In such a stance the teacher cannot be viewed as genuinely concerned with the success of each of his students. He develops tests that invariably catch even the brightest students—and the teacher satisfies himself that even the sharp character has a lot to learn. The tragedy is in the breakdown in the relationship between teacher and students.

The greatest fault of the status quo as it relates to the "sharp kid" is the self-deception into which it allows him to settle. As long as he can pull down the A's, cool the tests, and win the admiration of his peers, parents, and some teachers, he feels successful. The naked truth, however, may be that he is functioning far below his capabilities and developing habits that will prove difficult to overcome. His A's are not transferable to the competent performance needed for the solutions to real problems. He may have to step aside to allow another to take over the leadership—another who has demonstrated competence in a realistic manner. It is in such an experience that the straight-A student awakens to the reality that his education should have involved much more than the grade point average. His education should have required him to perform at his optimum ability at each succeeding level.

PLACING BLAME

At this point it becomes necessary to clarify a position. The reader may feel that the writers favor a soft, laissez-faire approach to the problems of education, in which the educator is to take the entire responsibility for the lack of student success. This just ain't so! We join others who may be tired of bearing the load of blame and guilt for the predicament of the world and of its struggling youth. Any time an older generation assumes all the responsibility, it is perpetrating a crime worse than it might imagine.

In short, our position is this: One of the prime responsibilities of parents and educators is that of building into the educational system a sense of responsibility on the part of each learner. Even further, it is a matter of developing an educational program that gives each student a series of opportunities that help him to develop a practical experience in bearing appropriate responsibilities. As he grows, he grows in his abilities to bear responsibility; he realizes that the rate of his growth and success is due, in large part, to his willingness to accept his personal share of obligation in learning experiences. It is our conviction that a large portion of our youthful population is willing and even anxious to do this.

It is our further conviction that the present system, the status quo, does not foster a sense of responsibility in young learners. Where any generalization is made, there are, of course, exceptions. There are teachers, and departments within the schools, whose philosophies and teaching styles bring to the student a sense of personal responsibility in the learning experience. But our basic premise is that this is the exception rather than the rule.

SICKNESS AT C LEVEL

We have looked at the traditional, graded system and its general history of failure in dealing with the needs of the slow learner, and we have seen that it has been equally ineffective in its relationship to the gifted learner. We now ask, "How about Mr. In-Between?" How effective is our present structure in educating the average student?

Here we have another problem: What or who is "average"? This is an elusive term used to cover too large a range. We are certain that within the large segment of "average" students there are a lot of unusual, unique, "un-average" people. They may have un-probed skills; and there is a chance that many average students are highly creative. But these students have been placed under the large canopy called average; it is within the framework of this admittedly inaccurate classification that we will examine the average student's predicament in the light of the present educational system.

Typically, the label "C student" or "average" tends to dampen the ardor or zeal of a student. Occasionally, an overachiever will buck the label, putting forth more than average effort to succeed. Such labels, however, ordinarily encourage a casual attitude toward scholastic requirements. As a result, the typical C student ends up in the role of an underachiever. Most could do better, but the effort is not worthwhile, and the penalties for underachieving are not severe enough to warrant concern. This lackadaisical attitude is further encouraged by the teacher who adjusts his requirements to the comfort of these average students. No one rocks the academic boat; the student remains floating comfortably at C level.

When graduation comes, the commencement speaker lauds the students for their successes and various accomplishments. He reminds them that they are the leaders of tomorrow. He tells them that they are better educated than any previous generation. They've spent more years in school, but the assertion is to be held in question. He emphasizes that their parents and teachers are proud of their attainments. The realistic teacher mumbles under his breath, "You've got to be kidding!" The concerned parent wonders if Joe or Mary can really cut it. And the student, hearing the praises and flattery, the promises and the hopes, has another reason to question the sincerity and integrity of the adult generation. He looks back to his past practices in school. To maintain his C level he has avoided those tougher courses that might have lowered his GPA. He has had the decency to keep from hurting his parents, but he has avoided areas of study that might have provided fascinating learning experiences. (We have witnessed incidents in which students contending for valedictorian honors have avoided courses that might lower the GPA.) Now he senses that he is not really prepared to face life—whether in the labor market, in the business world, or in the academic world. He knows that his letter grades are not marketable items; they do not signify that he has practical ability in any given area.

One area of security remains; his grade point average is the most accurate instrument for predicting his success in college. However, if he enters higher education with the same means for measuring success, the grade point average, he merely prolongs the uncertainty of his ability to succeed in the real world. There are countless college graduates who possess no identifiable marketable skills.

A COMPARISON

At the beginning of this chapter we asked questions about what may be wrong with our present educational system. We suggested, too, that a large number of great leaders have been developed in this country. These leaders, in the main, are products of our society and its school system. If our system is so bad, how can one account for the success of our great leaders?

In the first place, some will succeed in spite of the system. Second, no one (except possibly Admiral Rickover) would suggest that our schools are all bad. In fact, the American system and its endeavor to educate all American youth is one of the world's noblest educational efforts. The fact that education is not all bad may be illustrated by a physical fact of life. In our concern over air pollution today, we lash out at various industries that contribute heavily to the hazardous condition. In particular, we attack the auto industry—producer of high-powered internal combustion engines encased within the fancy-shaped automobiles that clutter the highways. The heavy brown curtain that veils the horizon leads us to cry out that something must be done. We hear the daily ozone reports on the number of parts of pollutants in the atmosphere. APCD (Air Pollution Control District) is as common a set of letters as were the WPA and the CCC of Depression days.

Occasionally we rise up in protest: We praise Ralph Nader, or we join a bicycle parade and ride down Main Street under the direction and surveillance of the tolerant local police. When our protest is over, we go back to driving our automobiles and continue to buy the products produced in those air-polluting industries. The cruel fact is that we cannot seem to get along without the automobile and numerous other products, but we could certainly get along without the pollution.

Few would compare traditional education with the modern automobile, but the parallel is not too remote. Like the automobile, it would be difficult to do without. And even though traditional education as we know it has been our principal means of (social) mobility, it still brings with it a number of high-powered ideas mingled with confusing and irritating conceptual smog. The numerous innovations, tacked on to the old educational system, merely decorate the exterior but do not get rid of the basic problems. When we were kids and added special strips of chrome to our cars, we knew that these additions didn't make the car run better. Basically, the numerous innovations set forth today do little more than what we did externally for our old "hot rods."

Not until we get into the basic mechanism, understand the principles of its functioning, and come up with improved or vastly changed parts will we produce an educational system that will meet society's and the learner's needs. But even more, not until we value this more humane and efficient concept of education will there be any significant change.

If all children of equal chronological age and equal academic ability are kept in the same grade for the same allotted time, we may still be working against the needs of a large number of children.

PLEASE, DON'T PASS THE HEMLOCK

3

As we gingerly step into this chapter, we would remind you of our basic premise while, at the same time, admitting a small problem.

PREMISES, PREMISES

First, the premise: It is our conviction that the continuous progress concept of education is basic to the effective, relevant education of our youth. Other innovations, to be effective, should move in the direction of providing opportunity for the continuous progress of each student.

Next, we have admitted that continuous progress education is not a new concept. Now, here comes the problem: In going back over its history, we find other terms or names given to this concept that we have chosen to call continuous progress. "So what?" you ask. "Where is the problem?" We find that these other terms are misleading to such an extent that they could have hindered the development (and likely did) of the concept.

UNRAVELING THE UNCLEAR

The problem of definition has kept the continuous progress concept of education under a fog of confusion. Not only has a clear definition been lacking, the concept has often been handicapped by negative names or titles. A practice cannot be brought into existence merely through a definition, yet a valid definition is needed to depict, in a proper light, the existence of a practice. Hence, we recommend critically reviewing the various terms and definitions applied to continuous progress.

From its inception, the concept of continuous progress education has been called "ungraded" or "nongraded" education; in some instances the term "individualized instruction" has been employed. Each of these labels is faulty or at least insufficient to convey the true meaning of continuous progress.

As we take a look at the term "nongraded" we see several faults. First, it is a negative term that does not depict a strong, positive program; one cannot see movement in any particular direction. It has the further disadvantage of being confusing; one cannot readily tell whether "nongraded" means that all grading systems (or marking systems) have been abolished, or whether grade levels (first, second, third) have been discontinued. And to some it may imply that all evaluation and classification of students has been discontinued. (If such were the case, there would be little means of determining progress of any kind, let alone determining continuous progress.)

From these initial misconceptions even more serious misunderstandings develop. For example, the negative term "nongraded" implies (in the minds of many) that structure and organization are missing from the classroom. The community, and parents in particular, may envision a loose conglomeration of meaningless activities selected at random, largely through the whims of the students. Such a setting smacks of the practice against which John Dewey himself warned. The parent who is concerned that his kids learn at least those basic tools that will help them to function in society and in the economic world has little patience with an ungraded situation in which he can recognize no definite plan. He views with suspicion many of these newfangled ideas promoted by the schools. Add to this the parent's inability to "figure this modern math," his concern over campus troubles, the inability of the school's product (the high school graduate) to function successfully in the labor market, and there is reason for the parent to long for the good old days or for the one-room schoolhouse and the schoolmarm who used the hickory stick to make the kids toe the line. It is thus likely that a fine concept of education may be rejected because it is either misunderstood, misrepresented, or both.

Even as the term nongraded is weak, negative, and misleading, so, too, is the term "ungraded"; hence, there is little reason to elaborate on its use.

OPEN AND SHUT CASES

Two other seemingly harmless terms implying innovative approaches need brief examination. One such term is "individualized instruction."

Closely associated with continuous progress, it stresses concern for the growth of the individual. It is a humane concept that places great value on each student. Individualized instruction involves careful diagnosis of student needs and abilities, it utilizes systematic evaluation procedures, and in it teachers use their skills to set up appropriate learning opportunities for the student.

However, individualized instruction **can** be misunderstood and it can imply mistaken concepts. Certain terrified teachers think of this term as meaning a one-to-one relationship with students throughout the day. They envision a task way beyond their physical and mental abilities. How can you deal with each individual personally throughout the day? In their panic, reason loses out to emotion, and the teachers reject the concept of individualized instruction as a highly theoretical and unworkable program. What they fail to realize is that individualized instruction can involve large groups and small groups of students. Not only **can** it involve student interaction, it **must** involve that important aspect of learning. Individualized instruction does not mean sticking each student into a cubicle or carrel, where he is to stay with the dedicated teacher hovering over him throughout the day. The fault, as we can see, lies partially in the term itself. The concept allows for far broader relationships and learning experiences than the term itself implies—the term suggests a restricted approach to teaching. This restriction, however, was never the intention of those educators who have promoted the consistent, individual development of each learner.

In recent years, the "open classroom" has been promoted as an approach that probes the needs and caters to the interests and abilities of the learner. It places a confidence and trust in the students' innate desire to learn.

Again misconceptions are rife. Inner walls of school buildings are removed so that there might be freedom of movement and flexibility of classroom arrangement. This initial step is hailed as the open classroom. But this renovation falls short of the real meaning of the term, for the teachers and administrators involved may still have a closed attitude toward the role of the teacher and the responsibilities of the students.

Inquirers are led to ask of the open classroom, "Open to what?" What constitutes openness? Could the proponents of the plan mean that various groups of learners are within view of each other? Does it mean that the activities are open to the choices of the students? Are there no plans and directions? The term "open classroom" may mean many things to many people, and it does not contribute to any significant clarification. Elements of individualization and opportunity for continuous student progress may be imbedded in the concept, but the term doesn't convey those possibilities.

A PEEK AT HISTORY

With these shortcomings in mind, we turn to a brief account of the development of continuous progress education. The noted historian Will Durant indicated that most of history is guessing and the rest is prejudice. With such a tongue-in-cheek definition of history, we could have little faith in our findings of the historical background of continuous progress education. We are not deeply concerned, however, with a definitive, highly researched study. It may be helpful, on the other hand, to look at a few historical facts in order to plan intelligently for the effective development of the continuous progress concept in the education of the future. Among the significant questions that may have been partially answered and some that still need answering are: Just how old or new is continuous progress education? How extensively was the principle adopted? At what levels in the educational scale has it been practiced most? How successful have these endeavors been? Were there any glaring faults in the programs instituted? What practices of the past would merit serious consideration in our plans for the future?

AN EARLY EXAMPLE

In seeking the origin of continuous progress learning, some would take us back to the early days of our country's history and to the one-teacher school. Certainly the seed or germ idea of continuous progress was found in such school settings. Children moved along in their learning, listened to the recitations of the older students, and didn't have to wait until the fourth grade before studying long division. If there was any lock step in the one-teacher school, at least the chairs weren't quite so tight and not so uniform in length.

It would be a mistake to go only to the past in reflecting on the one-teacher school. Many of our contemporaries have experienced such an educational setting. They have witnessed the one-teacher school, its cross-aged teaching in which older students help the younger, and the flexibility of time involved in the lessons and recitations. They've been left on their own to do the lessons, occasionally receiving help from the teacher or another student.

THE CEMENT HARDENS

With the comparatively new practice of consolidating schools and unifying school districts, educators have been better able to put students of the same chronological age together, to assign a teacher to a single grade, and to bring in a greater uniformity. Advocates of continuous progress education and individualized instruction hold that such a trend has taken us in the wrong direction. Let us illustrate.

Grouping in education should prove to be economical and efficient. However, grouping is usually done according to the chronological ages of the children. For social reasons, this may not be a bad idea. However, a room full of ten-year-olds may represent a broad continuum of students with varying abilities. Several of the ten-year-olds may not be ready for the tasks expected of the group. An equal number may have to mark time in such a class, for they may be ready for tasks beyond those expected of the group. If learning is the chief concern, then the educational efficiency of such a grouping is very low indeed. One suspects that where the educational efficiency is low, the economic efficiency is also low, especially if dollars are allocated on the basis of learning outcomes.

The larger schools are able to put the ten-year-old students in homogeneous groups, or in classes in which students have comparable learning abilities. This grouping appears to be more efficient, but it may (and likely will) be overlooking other important learning factors, including interests, needs, and motivation of students. If we take two students who are about equal in intellectual ability (if we dare, let us refer to the IQ) and in chronological age, we may find that one is highly motivated intrinsically while the other is not. We shall likely find that one has certain needs that the other does not have. One may be less mature physically than the other. The point should be obvious: there are many ways in which ten-year-olds might differ. Now, if all children of this equal chronological age and equal academic ability are kept in the same grade for the same allotted time (generally nine months), we may still be working against the individual needs of a large number of the children. In other words, the homogeneous group may be far more heterogeneous than homogeneous. In a grossly unfair illustration (unfair to the ten-year-old cherubs), we might take a look at thirty white pills: it would be dangerous to assume that all the pills are the same drug merely because they are the same size, shape, and color.

PLEASE, NO HEMLOCK

Continuous progress education seeks to identify the readiness of each learner in each area of learning. It seeks to begin at that point; to design learning opportunities that relate to the interests, needs, and abilities of each learner; and to allow the students to grow naturally by neither pushing them too fast nor holding them back. Generally, the learner is allowed to pursue the next challenge when he has demonstrated his competence and readiness through his performance. When a school or teacher has believed in and practiced this design for learning, there has been continuous progress education. By that definition, continuous progress education could well have antedated Socrates. Hopefully, the educational world has run out of hemlock.

PART TWO

THE COM PO NENTS

Guided by the teacher,
the student becomes a problem solver,
an investigator, a searcher for answers
to perplexing questions..

BUYING THE PACKAGE

4

Any program that involves interaction among people requires that decision making be guided by a philosophy. Furthermore, it seems almost too obvious to state that any plan of action is destined to go awry if competing or inimical philosophies are held by decision makers within the group. Otherwise well-planned efforts to initiate continuous progress programs have sometimes ended in disarray, leaving in their wake the misconception that the concept itself must have been unsound. Such unfortunate results can be unerringly predicted whenever any innovative program contains teachers who have not accepted the philosophy on which it is based. For the administrator to proceed under such conditions is to court disaster. Insofar as is humanly possible, the administrator should reassign, or make some other provisions for, teachers who are philosophically opposed to the concept of continuous progress. Developing new instructional methodologies is difficult at best, even for the teacher who is eager to do so and who is committed to the program. For the teacher who has neither the eagerness nor the commitment, every problem encountered, no matter how trivial, is seen as justification for the self-fulfilling prophecy of failure. Having a teacher in the program who is opposed to it makes about as much sense as having a crew member who wants to sink the ship.

Important as it is for all involved faculty members to be committed to the basic philosophy of continuous progress, it is just as necessary for boards of trustees, parents, administrators, and students not only to understand the concept but to accept it. If any one of these groups does not understand the philosophy, one may expect irritation among them when difficulties are experienced in the program. Long before the program is implemented in the schools, administrators and teachers should make every effort to enlist the understanding and support of all groups who are in any way involved with or interested in schools. Many board members and parents have conservative, traditional backgrounds in education, and the transition to a deep understanding and support of the continuous progress philosophy will not always be easy.

MAKING THE SHOE FIT

Why is it so difficult to accept a new philosophy, of education or of anything else? Like comfortable old shoes, a philosophy of education is often abandoned or changed with great reluctance. Once having changed one's philosophical shoes, however, one is quite likely to feel the pinch of the new ones when walking too rapidly down the path of innovation, and one may be tempted to return to the psychological comfort of traditionalism.

Why is it so difficult to abandon a traditional philosophy of education? Perhaps because the traditionalism of most educators has long been based on a triad of concepts that we identify with the acronym SAP. These concepts are:

1. Sanctity of grade levels as the basis for organizing instruction.
2. Agonizing attempts to cover the material, whether or not the students understand it.
3. Practice of evaluating student progress by comparison with other students.

This triad has dominated education practice for so long that many people have thoughtlessly accepted the philosophy without inquiring as to its justification. Naturally, any self-respecting traditionalist knows you've got to organize schools into grade levels, otherwise you wouldn't know who is ready to graduate. And if you didn't have graduations, what would the American Legion do with all those awards to outstanding young citizens? And you must, just absolutely must, finish with those books by June because a new bunch of kids is going to need them in September. And, as anybody knows, you must identify the A students and the F students; otherwise their parents wouldn't know which kid to be proud of!

Although the term "philosophy" may be high-sounding, even formidable to some, everybody has some sort of a guiding operational philosophy, even though he may not be able to verbalize it clearly. Simply put, a philosophy is a matrix of beliefs that guides a person's decisions and hence his or her actions. Anytime people are engaged in a common pursuit, they must function in terms of a common philosophy if they are to achieve common ends. This acceptance of a common philosophy involves more than a verbal or even intellectual assent. Any philosophy is the rational outgrowth of a core of essential beliefs that must be held as prerequisite ingredients to the fully developed philosophy. However willing one might be to accept the continuous progress philosophy, one's attempts to implement that philosophy in the classroom will fail unless one is firmly committed to the fundamental core of beliefs.

DOWN TO THE HARD CORE

We would be the first to agree that many fine teachers have held some of the beliefs we are specifying as prerequisites. And we are not so bold or so naive as to suggest that these beliefs present anything new on the educational scene. What we are saying is that **in toto** they constitute the foundation of the continuous progress philosophy. Without holding these beliefs, the teacher is intellectually, and therefore operationally, unable to implement the continuous progress philosophy. We have identified seven beliefs that, in our opinion, constitute that essential core. If you have identified others, we certainly will not quarrel with you. Ours can be labeled as follows:

1. Worth of the individual.
2. A philosophy of the humane in education.
3. Individual differences.
4. Within a structure, freedom of choice.
5. Student responsibility for his or her own learning.
6. The teacher as director of learning.
7. The educator's need for professional freedom.

We will now describe each of these aspects in more detail and explain why they are so important.

Worth of the Individual

This concept requires belief in the right of students to have their own opinions and even to have the opportunity to choose among alternate learning activities presented by the teacher. It requires the teacher not to coerce the student but to present all sides of an issue for consideration. Undoubtedly, no teacher would admit to not believing in the worth of the individual. In our democracy we all give lip service to this concept, but the actions of some teachers belie their benevolent verbalizations.

Homogeneous grouping is seen by many as an expression of belief in the worth of the individual. However, no group is ever truly homogeneous. There are always students whose intellectual ability does not permit them to keep pace with those in their own group. Anxiety, frustration, cumulative retardation, and sometimes failure await the slow learner whose performance is evaluated in terms of his peers instead of his own potential. Belief in the worth of the individual would preclude this educational treatment of any learners. Even within a given ability group, why should a student have to achieve in terms of a group norm? Belief in the inherent worth of a homogeneous group seems to be what many teachers practice, despite what they preach.

If one's belief in the worth of the individual is strong enough to affect one's methods in the classroom, it will affect everything from the tone of one's voice to the measures one employs in maintaining classroom control. We do not mean to imply that teachers should adopt a silly, Pollyanna sentimentalism in dealing with students, but continuous progress does require a teacher mode that never violates the dignity of the student. At times a stern command may be indicated, but even this can be administered without demeaning the student's individual worth. Lines have to be drawn, limits set; but such direction does not require sarcasm, cynicism, or any other response that robs the individual of his inherent human dignity before his peers.

A Philosophy of the Humane in Education

The concept of the humane in education is inseparable from the concept of the worth of the individual, yet the idea of the humane does present some additional facets for consideration. The humane includes many qualities, including kindness, tenderness, mercy, and consideration—in short, the humanizing qualities. Recognizing that many teachers do exhibit these qualities in their interactions with students, we must still note that there are many teachers who do not. Perhaps a closer look at these four qualities of the humane will be in order.

First, in examining the definition of the word "kindness," we will skip over the commonly understood meaning of a sympathetic or generous quality. Instead, we will turn to the primary meaning of the word "kind" as referring to the origin or nature of beings, as in "after one's kind." Thus, a precise understanding of this quality implies recognition of the common origin of the teacher and the student—co-sharers of the human predicament, though with different status, to be sure! Recognition of this "kind"-ness should make it easier for the teacher under stress to display the sympathetic and generous qualities commonly understood to be subsumed in the term "kindness."

Second, to many teachers and parents the term "tenderness" may seem appropriate for the teacher who is the parent-surrogate in the primary grades but highly out of place in the auto shop or the chemistry lab! We would agree that many school situations do call for firm, unyielding discipline, with a no-nonsense adherence to well-established rules and policies. But we hold that even when the teacher must say to the student, "You broke the rule and must suffer the consequences of your own actions," the humane teacher can exercise this authoritarian function within a framework of kindness, tenderness, and a complete absence of any feeling of revenge or satisfaction at having caught a culprit. We categorically reject for "tenderness," in this context, the idea of the misty-eyed softy who lacks the courage to function in a proper teacher role.

The third quality of the humane is that of "mercy." In our context, mercy is "kindness in excess of what may be expected or demanded by fairness." Does this, too, sound out of place as a possible teacher response? We have seen teachers who were so uptight about justice that they had little time for, or understanding of, mercy. This justice syndrome is always one of reaction: The student acts (inappropriately) and the teacher reacts. Reaction typically requires little thought or creativity. It is simply a response to a given stimulus. To initiate action requires a qualitatively different response, on a higher order than reaction. For the teacher to elect to exercise mercy in a disciplinary situation requires enlightened initiative because, admittedly, its use must be selective and based on the uniqueness of the situation. Rather than an either-or posture with justice and mercy at opposite ends of the pole, we prefer an intelligent, well-blended interaction of the two responses. Our plea is against the legalistic outlook that is blind to the possibility of mercy as an option.

"Consideration" is the fourth quality subsumed in the concept of the humane. It is simply a thoughtful regard for the feelings of others. This thoughtful regard does not imply avoidance of discipline. On the contrary, a thoughtful regard may be the teacher's most impelling motive for taking disciplinary action. Consideration for the student's feelings implies only that the teacher will use good judgment and tact in the mode and circumstances of administering discipline.

In an era when assassination of three national figures is a **fait accompli** and assassination of others has been attempted, we are not apologetic for stressing the need for the humane as a basic tenet for educators. If the teacher is not humane in relationships with students, there is little to be expected from the teaching of humaneness as a concept. Is it too much to hope that if every student in America were to experience the humane in education, the day would come when the noncerebral reactions of vengeance and violence would give way to the more creative actions of the truly humane person?

Individual Differences

No teacher is likely to argue against the fact that differences in learning ability exist from one individual to another or to say that these differences are unimportant. Yet despite the past decade of intense efforts to develop a methodology of teaching that is superior to the prevalent mode, successful innovative practices are like little islands of creativity in a sea of traditionalism. One fundamental reason for this incongruous state of affairs is that although most teachers have an intellectual commitment to the doctrine of individualization of instruction, many of them are not sufficiently committed to it to cause them to endure the hassle of pushing for change in a district that may not be change oriented. Furthermore, a great many teachers honestly believe that individualization of instruction can be accomplished within the framework of a grade-level type of organization. So they may work away, either in isolation or with small groups of colleagues, trying to deal with individual differences in a traditional setting that is inimical to their goals.

It is our belief that no teacher can, or will care to, succeed in a continuous progress program unless enthusiastically committed to individualization of both the teaching and the learning process. A teacher who is not thus committed will not only fail in his or her own efforts but will tend to undermine the entire program. The teacher who prefers relating to a class-size group is not likely to invest the time and energy required to function in a school where the common mode is either individual or small-group interaction. Hence, we see the teacher's firm belief in individual differences as absolutely essential to the acceptance of the philosophy of continuous progress.

Within a Structure, Freedom of Choice

Certain disciplines are inherently sequential. Prior concepts form the basis for understanding subsequent concepts. Obviously, in such disciplines the learning sequence is important. But outside these areas students should have freedom to decide what interests them most and what they wish to pursue. For example, the sequence of the social sciences typically offered at the secondary level is largely meaningless. On what basis may we say that World History must be followed by U.S. History, and finally by U.S. Government? Once we are prepared to live with the concept that literature, for instance, might be profitably studied before or even without grammar, we should be prepared to offer the students considerable freedom, not only in the selection of courses that interest them but in the choice of learning activities designed to promote that learning. To deny students the right to choose, within limits, what they wish to study, or to deny them the right to select those activities that seem to them likely to promote the desired learning, is to deny the fundamental concept of continuous progress. Some may object that the student may not be in a position to choose wisely either the subject he or she should study or the learning activities appropriate to that subject. To this objection we would reply that mistakes are sometimes the most effective teachers.

Obviously, we do not recommend letting the student sink in the quagmire of endless, unguided floundering. It is the teacher's responsibility to offer guidance and suggestions at appropriate times.

To offer direction so as to prevent students from making valid choices based on their interests is to forfeit one's right to membership in the continuous progress fraternity—(or sorority, as the case may be).

Student Responsibility for His or Her Own Learning

For decades educators (with some exceptions, of course) have acted as though the responsibility for learning lies entirely with the teacher. The student's responsibility has been seen as that of getting to school and following directions. From there on it is the teacher's ball game. This approach has made the teacher responsible for deciding:

1. What and how much should be learned when and by whom.
2. What experiences or activities would most suitably promote the desired learning.
3. How much time should be allotted to any given task.
4. What criteria should be used for evaluating pupil progress.
5. What constitutes failure.

This relegates the student to the role of: "Yours not to question why; yours but to do or die" (grade-wise anyhow!). And this in a society whose educational system is supposedly committed to the development of initiative and decision-making skills in each generation! Little wonder that the passivity of the students' role leaves many of them disinterested, apathetic, and sometimes belligerent. Like a car with its motor running and its clutch disengaged, they may race their motors and make a lot of noise, but they seldom get anywhere—unless it's downhill!

The only decision really open to the student is whether to comply with or to rebel against the school. If a student opts for rebellion, nonparticipation in the school program is usually part of the syndrome. Even the decision as to whether or not to come to school in the first place is not really his, since attendance is required by law. The significant decisions about the educational program are made **for** the student, not **by** the student. This arrangement leaves ample incentive to criticize the teacher if the student fails or refuses to learn. Defensive parents are quick to lay the blame at the teacher's door, especially when the rules of the game are made by the teacher and when goals and objectives are not specified as criteria for evaluation of pupil performance.

When we propose that the student be responsible for his or her own learning, we do not visualize classrooms without teachers, or students making decisions that ought to be made by teachers. We recognize that many decisions can only be made by teachers, but it is our view that some of the decisions commonly made for students would be better made by them. Obviously, the organization of curriculum content is the teacher's responsibility, but at the level of the student's daily work, why could he not be presented with a number of learning activities from which to choose? Each of the activities might be designed to promote the same learning, but each student could pursue the goal by engaging in an activity of his own choice. There might be only two or three alternatives, but it would still enable each student to exercise an option.

Any teacher can tell you how rough goes the day when the planned learning activities happen not to interest the students. If we may paraphrase a bit, it can be said with certainty that hell hath no fury like the pent-up wrath of a bored class. A sure-fire way of capturing students' interest is to give them, from time to time, the wheel of their own educational ship and let them chart their own course for a while under the eye of an experienced and knowledgeable skipper. A few less-than-brilliant choices are not likely to sink the ship. All things considered, we are by no means prepared to concede that some student mischoices would necessarily retard the student's progress. The exhilaration of having some autonomy is more likely to accelerate the educational process than to deter it. Poor choices might delay it slightly, but the educational race is not necessarily to the swift.

Another advantage of providing choices for students is that the simple act of choosing a particular learning activity provides the student with a feeling of commitment and a responsibility to justify his choice by bringing the activity to a successful conclusion.

Equally important is the new psychological equation that comes into being between the student and the teacher when the teacher drops the role of omniscience, begins to function as a resource person, and lets the student assume some control over his own learning. It is axiomatic that the privilege of making choices carries with it the obligation to complete the activity or assignment chosen. All of a sudden, the monkey is off the teacher's back and onto the student's. Once the student has made some choices about his own educational activities, the old "dare-ya-to-teach-me-something" syndrome is completely negated. Instead of the alignment of teacher versus student, with the teacher always in a superordinate position, the new relationship is one of partnership. To be sure, the teacher is the senior partner, but the relationship is a working one, with the student initiating and carrying out the work and the teacher being ready for consultation, suggestions, and explanations whenever needed. Most teachers who have functioned in this role greatly prefer it to the traditional one. This teacher role is certainly preferable wherever possible, and it is our contention that it is possible in the majority of cases. It would be naive to assume that the continuous progress program will result in all students becoming self-actualizers who assume the initiative for planning their educational experiences. We do not make that assumption. We do, however, assert our belief that a surprising number of students will do precisely that in response to the stimulation of participating in the decisions that affect their learning and of assuming responsibility for their own progress. For those students who either cannot or do not respond to such opportunities, the traditional role of the teacher as catalyst, resource person, guide, and the putter-on-of-pressure is still not only valid but inescapable.

The Teacher as the Director of Learning

Formal education was, until very recently, product oriented. By this we mean that the goal of education was the production of completely educated persons who had endured the rigors of the system, mastered everything the school had to offer, and were proudly presented to the world as the products of the educational system. It was assumed that whatever knowledge was of worth had been transferred from the teacher to the student.

Among other assumptions of this approach was the idea that there exists a body of knowledge and tradition essential for survival and productive living. It was assumed that learned men were in possession of this knowledge and that its transmission to each generation was the goal of education.

Another interesting assumption was that the mind of an uneducated person is like a tabula rasa simply waiting to be filled with the appropriate facts. Also implicit in this thinking was the notion that the teacher was the ultimate authority on educational matters and that the proper stance for the learner was that of an innocent novice sitting at the feet of the scholar. The proper role of the teacher was to impart information to students, while the proper role of students was to respectfully and unquestioningly assimilate facts.

In 1592, when Francis Bacon said in a letter to Lord Burghley, "I have taken all knowledge to be my province," he could at worst have been accused of arrogance. True, he laid out for himself, even in his day, an impressive province but not one that was patently impossible. But in today's context of the knowledge explosion, a statement such as Bacon's would be prima facie evidence of lunacy. With knowledge presently doubling every decade, no one can hope to learn all there is to be known, even in a specialty within a discipline.

This exponential rate of increase of knowledge has made earlier assumptions about education as useless as landing gear on a goldfish. It has also drastically altered the role of the teacher in the education process. Whereas the teacher was formerly regarded as the source of all knowledge, he is now regarded as a director of the learning process. Whereas he was formerly viewed as the living embodiment of wisdom, he is now viewed as an adviser, a consultant who can facilitate the learning process by suggesting learning activities, sources of information, and alternate approaches to problem solving. The teacher is now viewed as a designer of learning experiences, as an evaluator of the extent to which learning has occurred, and as a diagnostician of learning difficulties. Having shed his aura of omniscience, the teacher no longer needs to dread that awful moment when he is forced to say, "I don't know" in response to a student's question. For now that it is no longer possible for anyone, not even a teacher, to know everything, there is no disgrace in admitting to being human. But since the teacher's new role is that of consultant and adviser, he would be well advised to help students find answers to their questions—particularly the questions whose answers the teacher himself does not know. We are not condoning ignorance or poor academic preparation on the part of the teachers. Naturally they should be well informed in their disciplines. We are merely emphasizing the impossibility of learning everything and the need to accept the human fallibility of teachers.

Clearly, then, the era of The Product as the goal of education has come belatedly to its end. We concede that one can still find schools aplenty where the product orientation is in vogue, but happily their numbers are decreasing and their adherents are on the defensive. Product orientation has made way for process orientation. Which is to say that since it is no longer possible to learn everything, we must accept the goal of helping all students to master the learning process. Along with this mastery, the student must develop an attitude that favors learning throughout the rest of his life.

Why is this attitude essential for the meaningful survival of contemporary human beings? The exponential rate of increase of knowledge that has rendered total learning an impossibility has also created a society characterized by such rapid change that many of the vocations that will occupy people ten years from now do not exist today. By the time a person graduates from college, half of what he or she was taught in the sciences is already obsolete. Under such conditions, the only defensible goal for education is to teach students the process of learning so that they can successfully cope with constantly accelerating change throughout their lives. We do not in any way mean to diminish the importance of learning fundamental skills and of mastering a discipline. We do, however, want to point out that no one can ever again rightfully put a period to the educational product. Never again can the educated person retire from the pursuit of knowledge. The pursuit is not necessarily to the swift, but it is certainly to the persistent. The philosophy of process orientation does not advocate teaching a process that encourages future learning but neglects the present need to master a discipline. On the contrary, process orientation places great emphasis on mastery of fundamental skills as well as vocational skills (or an academic discipline) as a prime requisite for the person who aspires to lifelong learning in an era of exploding knowledge.

The person who is process oriented rather than product oriented tends to be adaptable. In the decades ahead, during which it appears that the only constant will be change—and change at an accelerating rate—adaptability seems likely to be prerequisite not only to success but to survival. The product-oriented learner who tends to put periods after all his assertions rather than question marks and who ends all his cerebral "chapters" with unequivocal dogmatisms is likely to find that his intellectual attainments are in little demand in a culture that is so busy peering into the rapidly expanding future that it has little time to ponder the past. On the other hand, the process-oriented individual finds his adaptability much in demand because he is skilled in the processes of learning and is not stymied by new concepts or techniques. His intellectual modus vivendi predisposes him to being constantly in touch and in tune with the new. He functions optimally at the cutting edge of current developments, and effective accommodation to change becomes a natural part of his life style.

The interaction between students and teachers is so interdependent that it is difficult to discuss the changing role of the teacher without also discussing the changing role of the student. Since the teacher is no longer regarded as the primary source of information, the student is no longer viewed as an empty receptacle to be filled passively with whatever data the teacher decides are appropriate and useful. Guided by the teacher, to be sure, the student becomes a problem solver, an investigator, a searcher for answers to questions that perplex him. It is the function of the teacher to guide the student, to motivate him, so that wherever possible the areas of his quests will coincide with the requirements that he must meet. There will be instances in which this happy congruence of interests and requirements will not occur. In such cases the student will simply have to endure the maturational phenomenon of doing what has to be done even in the absence of an overpowering curiosity or an insatiable interest. It is a professional cop-out, however, if the teacher takes constant refuge behind requirements and never succeeds in stimulating curiosity, piquing a latent interest, or bolstering waning zeal with a well-timed mention of a source of information the student has been unable to locate.

Implementing the proper roles for teacher and student puts them on the same side of the desk. Often they are co-investigators. It is not completely unthinkable that the teacher sometimes becomes a learner from one of his or her students. If such an intellectual symbiosis seems like educational heresy to you, or like robbing the teacher of the authoritarian role, or like something else you don't like, you might think about some alternatives—such as bored students, sullen confrontations, or teachers with ulcers.

The Educator's Need for Professional Freedom
The concepts that make up the continuous progress philosophy require that educators be allowed freedom to exercise their professional judgment in developing programs to meet the diverse needs

of students. It is stating the obvious to say that these concepts must always guide the day-to-day implementation of the philosophy as it is worked out in individual programs. Nevertheless, this needs to be said in order to counteract the teacher's natural tendency to regress in subtle ways toward the comfort of the accustomed mean in organizing instruction.

One of the concepts that must be kept in mind is that of the school as a center of inquiry. Inquiry is generated by intellectual curiosity and is a highly individualistic process. In interacting with students in this process, teachers, too, must function in highly individualistic ways that are the reciprocals of input and feedback received from students. Teachers must be diagnosticians of students' learning difficulties, prescribers of remedial measures, empathizers with students and their sometimes half-formed concepts, and evaluators of the student's achievement—or lack of achievement—of stated objectives. Sometimes teachers find themselves in an even more challenging and stimulating role as participants with their students in the age-old search for knowledge. In this role the teacher is a model of the continuous learner and is in the happy condition of practicing what he preaches. These interactions can flourish only in an atmosphere of responsible freedom.

Teachers must feel secure in the constant quest for better means of accomplishing these ends. They can feel this security only if they have the assurance that they will not be punished for the inevitable failures that occasionally occur in the complex process of structuring new learning experiences. Talk is, indeed, cheap, and teachers will need more than verbal assurance if they are to feel free to be creative and to act often on mere hunches as they design educational experiences for students, many of whom have deep-seated learning difficulties.

The kinds of punishment to which a teacher may be subtly subjected as a means of showing official disapproval are many. The principal or supervisor who worships at the shrine of a quiet classroom, and whose beaming approval is in direct proportion to the educational equivalent of "A Stillness at Appomattox," is exhibiting an often noncerebral bias that is evidence of an inadequate understanding of the concepts of individualization. We do not mean to imply that individualized programs generate noisy classrooms. Often, precisely the opposite is true, as students, sometimes for the first time, become engrossed in learning experiences that have personal significance for them.

Administrators who strive to provide a nonthreatening environment for developing innovative programs must do more than say they are nonthreatening. They must demonstrate repeatedly, under the tension of actual classroom situations, that they are supportive and nonjudgmental in the face of classroom interactions that present new problems with which to cope. If they succeed in demonstrating to their faculties that it actually is safe for them to try and to fail, the creative potential released will provide the needed impetus for further innovative ventures.

The individualization of learning experiences has many implications for the principal as the instructional leader of the school. He, too, must be granted sufficient autonomy to make judgments about every aspect of the program. It must be recognized that the continuous progress program that emerges in one school must not be expected to be a carbon copy of such programs in other schools, even within the same district. The basic philosophy should be identical in all programs if, in fact, the philosophy is defensible. But since individualization is the very heart of the philosophy, that philosophy itself recognizes the necessity of differences in implementation to the extent that cultural, social, and economic differences are found in different communities. Therefore, within the broad conceptual framework of continuous progress, and within an equally broad district philosophy, the principal must be allowed the prerogative of developing cooperatively with his faculty a program that is fitted to the needs of pupils in that particular community.

It is not by accident that we use such terms as "emerging" and "developing" here. The whole concept of continuous progress education is so diametrically opposed to the traditional lock step system that teachers and students alike will require time to become skilled at functioning within the new frame of reference. Students, faculty, and parents must work together to refine and perfect continuous progress education. This requirement has important implications for the relationship between teachers and administrators— particularly the school principal. Principals and other administrators must help teachers to redefine their relationships with students. The new methodology makes many demands on teachers. They must become comfortable in the new role of consultant, adviser, and designer of learning experiences. This is not an easy accomplishment, especially if they have relied heavily on the role of authoritarian dispenser of answers.

Although the bounds of propriety will be maintained in the new teacher-student relationship, this relationship will almost unavoidably become more informal. This does not mean that it will become disrespectful; in fact, we see no essential tension between the concepts of respectfulness and informality. The resultant informality is an inherent concomitant of the individualized and often self-planned learning activities of the student. When students function as self-actualizing individuals rather than as passive components of a group, there is bound to be a resultant informality in the learning environment. Administrators must recognize this situation and be prepared to let teachers try the unknown, letting experience, rather than administrative edict, be the basis for deciding the usefulness of various procedures.

The enthusiastic innovator is often impatient with the slow-moving machinery that results when the community is brought into the planning.

CALLING THE VILLAGERS TO A TOWN COUNCIL

5

If educators were to adopt Ralph W. Tyler's rationale for curriculum development, and there are sound reasons for doing so, they would bring into consideration three sources for the development of educational objectives: (1) the student, (2) the society, and (3) the subject.

If Tyler's rationale were adopted, the almost inane arguments between the promoters of student-centered and subject-centered curricula would hopefully cease. Such debates have been arguments for imbalance. Both subject-centered and student-centered concepts of curriculum are too restrictive, and both viewpoints lead their proponents to embrace positions that neglect educational practices of major significance. It is surprising, on analysis, to see brilliant educational leaders lining up on one side or the other to embrace one of these restrictive viewpoints.

MAKE WAY FOR THE PARENTS

Few educators would set forth a parent-centered curriculum. Labels would be slapped on such educators in much the same way that the suitcase of a world traveler is covered with stickers of the exotic places to which the suitcase and its owner have journeyed. In this case, however, the labels would not be flattering—authoritarian, inhumane, and outmoded would be three of the least offensive tags. Yet the parent-centered curriculum might be as defensible as either of the other two. The following arguments could be given in support of a parent-centered curriculum:

1. The honest parent certainly has a very real concern for the student's future and for his or her present welfare.
2. The life experience of the parent is of some value. Even though the now generation occasionally relegates the opinions and experiences of parents to the past, the fact remains that the living parent may have as much awareness of relevant issues and facts as does the youth or the learned professor.
3. The investment of parents, and society in general, adds the dimension of accountability to curricular planning. This concern is not altogether negative; it not only involves caution in educational expenditures, but it also reveals a concern for the educational development of the learner.
4. Many parents have sufficient time combined with an active interest in education to be of real assistance in educational planning.
5. The values of the parent and of the society should not be ignored or set aside. These values, given careful consideration, help give direction and purpose to the curriculum.

It is not our intent to set forth a brief in behalf of a parent-centered curriculum; the point to be made is merely that the arguments supporting student-centered or subject-centered curricula are scarcely more valid than the argument for a parent-centered curriculum.

An additional point needs to be given consideration; Tyler's rationale, with its three sources for developing educational objectives, allows for individual differences. It does not pour every student or teacher into the same mold. With the differences of style existing among the teachers, and the countless interests of the students, each can place emphasis on special strengths or concerns—that is, as long as a reasonable balance is maintained and reasonable respect is shown toward all three sources. The rationale involves a balance of three factors—students, subject, and society.

COMMUNITY INVOLVEMENT

In planning innovative curricula, the parent and the larger society (the constituency of the school) should play a significant role. The curriculum innovator who ignores this segment is inviting failure—even disaster.

The enthusiastic innovator is often impatient with the slow-moving machinery that results when the community is brought into the planning. The innovator must not, however, ask how he can avoid this barrier to progress. Rather, he should ask, "How can the community become an effective factor in curriculum planning?"

Here we would introduce the "Five I's of Innovation" as the task of innovation relates to the community. These I's are: (1) Inform, (2) Inquire, (3) Invite, (4) Involve, and (5) Interact.

IGNORE SOME I'S

There are some I's that need to be tossed out. Among these are "Indulge" and "Insist." An intelligent community, and we must assume that the community is intelligent, will recognize the game playing of an innovator who merely indulges the community with bits of information and with token roles in the planning. Such indulgence will breed distrust. And it will reveal to the community that the innovator is not absolutely confident of the direction he is recommending; if he were, his plans would bear up under careful scrutiny.

Nor will it take the community long to react negatively to the innovator who insists on following certain procedures. It is in such cases that the community digs in its heels. The insister also betrays a lack of confidence in the community. He is telling the community that he knows what is good for it, that he is informed in areas in which the community has relatively little information.

THE I'S THAT HAVE IT

The Five I's of Innovation need to be taken as a package. Whereas each "I" is an important segment, no one of them is sufficient by itself to be a significant factor in the innovator's relationship to the community. Neither is it possible to place them in the order of their importance or in an exact sequence of steps. The Five I's need to be viewed as the cumulative task of the innovator who would successfully involve the community in curriculum planning. Because of the limitations of written communication, we will treat them as individual, discreet actions to be employed by the innovator.

Inform

The task of informing the community cannot be overemphasized. And here we must insist on informing with integrity. The innovator must be careful of the following:

1. He must not give only partial information. This practice is deceptive. When the community discovers this condition, its confidence is destroyed. The innovator can expect an immediate loss of support.
2. If the innovator merely informs the community of what the school is doing, or of what it is planning to do, he is

indulging in a highly unsatisfactory procedure. He does not involve the community; he merely tells the community that it is not involved, or that it is only informationally involved (if such can be called involvement).

Correct procedure for informing the community accomplishes a minimum of two objectives. First, it makes the community aware of the general direction in which educational practices are going. Key issues of education, with their pros and cons, are passed on to the community.

Second, the innovator conveys to the community the educational direction that he is interested in pursuing. This information should be accompanied by sufficient reasons for the plan under consideration. The innovator should show that his approach may best meet the needs, interests, and the abilities of the students involved.

Equally important is the **how** of transmitting the information. The reader can probably think of several means for transmitting information to the community: (1) the news media, most likely the local newspaper, (2) the P.T.A., (3) school open house, (4) the school paper, (5) special school-community functions, (6) local clubs and business organizations, (7) brochures, either printed or mimeographed, and (8) the various opportunities for direct communication.

The innovator should keep in mind that regardless of the effectiveness of some of these media for communicating information, none is more effective than face-to-face communication. Most other means, even the most attractive informational approaches, leave some questions unanswered and much to be desired. Memos are sometimes irritating, written reports are often inaccurate, and other means not involving direct personal communication are frequently too general and vague. It should be apparent that there are few substitutes for direct communication.

Inquire

Unilateral communication in innovative endeavors is not sufficient. Would-be innovators must not only inform the community but inquire of the community. This inquiry must be sincere, with the purpose of implementing those concepts that may be vital to curricular improvement. This inquiry of the community must probe community interest, needs, ideas, attitudes, readiness, talents, awareness, and willingness to be involved.

The right questions, accompanied by a sincere desire to discern the climate of the community, can reap a rich harvest of ideas, attitudes, and concerns. These sources cannot be ignored when innovations are planned.

Invite

Logically, on the heels of an honest inquiry into the community's thoughts come certain invitations to this same community.

The community, at least that segment that has a definite interest and that has shown an active response, may be invited to view present practices at the school and in other districts. It may be invited to discuss basic plans and their alternatives. It may be invited to be on committees, which may be authorized to draw up proposals in several areas—proposals for informing the entire community, proposals for a course of action, proposals for implementation.

Involve

As suggested earlier, these Five I's are not distinct or discreet; they fuse into one attitude—one basic relationship between innovator and community. Thus, any invitation extended to the community is an invitation to that community to become involved.

An involved community is quite likely to become a committed community. Seldom will an individual or group of people become actively engaged in a project or in an investigation of a project without becoming positively committed to an idea. It is almost inconceivable how one could spend considerable time and energy, especially voluntarily, without coming to identify oneself with a point of view. Casual unconcern would seldom accompany such involvement. This does not mean, however, that the participants will necessarily identify positively with the proposals of the innovator. The wise innovator would not want to insist upon such a sheeplike following.

Involvement takes several forms. Basically, whatever the involvement, the individuals in the community should participate in the area of their strengths, their interests, and their unique talents. Surveys, committees, evaluative studies, and special research tasks are but a few of the many activities in which individuals of the community might be utilized.

Interact

Healthy involvement will bring about a vigorous interaction among the participants. It does not mean an immediate identification of loyalties or sides in the issue. Clear thinking may seem to be accompanied by early confusion, but it is merely a matter of getting inputs and relating these inputs to various factors and premises. Decision makers may drop ideas, return to ideas, and change positions based on the growing evidence garnered through the input contributions made by the committee members.

The leader in these interactive experiences, regardless of the social level of the community involved, must allow for genuine interaction. Any undue pressures that would quell or discourage the expression of ideas would establish a repressive climate. The simplest ideas of the humblest citizen should be aired and respected.

SEEING I TO I

We would certainly hope that the innovator might have the "eyes of the wise," that he or she might have the insight to incorporate the Five I's of Innovation. The one who lacks insight will be the one who tends to incite negative reactions to even potentially worthwhile ideas.

Successful innovation, as it relates to the community,
Informs
Inquires
Invites
Involves
Interacts

And we suspect that an intelligent, innovative thrust may do something even greater—it might just inspire individuals and the community to action that will truly instruct.

Boredom is the plague of youthful minds in the relatively unchallenging environment of the traditional classroom.

FROM THE EYE OF THE PUPIL

6

Even though students may express boredom over the dull experiences of school, the tack of suddenly introducing them to something different may be unwise. The innovator who bathes the youth in the cold water of something totally new, may himself be shocked with the reaction from the students.

There are educators who view the young as basically conservative and oriented toward the traditional. This view is not without supportive evidence. For example, students are known to offer resistance to new approaches that may not appear to give them the necessary background for college. At times, when teachers alter past procedures, or when they treat students differently from the way former students (or "the other kids") were treated, students react vocally and persistently. These reactions are not merely against the unfairness of a change, but against the change itself. Even the young can rather quickly settle into a comfortable rut. It is possible that the students may enjoy the privilege of griping about the existing monotony of the current practice far more than they would the shock of a major change for which they have not been prepared.

Our basic premise, therefore, is that innovation should not be rudely thrust upon the student any more than upon teachers or the adults of the community. The innovation should be introduced to the student with its purposes, its advantages, its problems, its opportunities, and its overall rationale.

A TIME FOR CONFESSION

Our problem is simply set forth: Just what should be done to prepare the students for a new thrust in education?

The **first** step is a basic acknowledgement. Perhaps a harder term is confession. If a proposal for change is presented to students, it must, obviously, be a change to a better program. The inquiring student will need to be satisfied with honest answers. The current or past program has not been satisfactory. It has not provided for the full potential of the learner. It may be too brittle, having met the needs of only a small segment of the student group. Any of a large number of shortcomings may be true of the curriculum that is due for a change. The most overused term in condemning any practice is "relevance." The curriculum has not been relevant. Such may be the case, but criticism couched in relevance-irrelevance terms may itself be rejected; conservative thinkers do not like to have their experiences or positions shot down by an overused word, phrase, or slogan.

Another caution with regard to this first step of acknowledging that the current curriculum has been inadequate is that the innovator must not portray the past or present practices as all bad. Realistically, this could not be the case, for it would be highly unlikely that the community would be totally entrapped by such an evil approach. If the innovator were to print such a bleak picture of the practice he would change, he would lose the confidence of most reflective thinkers—and there are such thinkers among the young. Any case of oversell would end up in overkill.

A very real confession or acknowledgement, then, of present inadequacies in educational practices, while not condemning all that is being done, can be the first step toward effective change.

An educational practice must be viewed as inadequate if it does not provide for the development of the full potential of each student. If it provides for or challenges only a segment of the student group, it is inadequate. If it is designed to meet the needs of all the students but doesn't make provision for the full potential within each, it is still inadequate. This evaluation may seem idealistic and unreal in the minds of many, but any provision based on a lesser goal is tragic. "Provision for the full potential" does not mean that the full potential will be actualized in each student. The learner must bear his responsibility in the learning experience. If this point is not acknowledged by parents and students, the school will always be at fault. Continuous pampering and continuous prodding do not necessarily go hand in hand with continuous progress.

The **second** step is to accent clearly the purpose of the curricular direction being recommended. When the student perceives the purpose of what he is doing, he becomes a more successful student. In fact, an understanding of the purpose in any undertaking has definite advantages:

1. The perceived purpose gives the student a head start in the task of learning. A learner will have more difficulty learning "nonsense syllables" than he will those symbols that have meaning and that have a useful place in a meaningful design. Most of us have taken courses that have been little more than "nonsense syllables" at best. We had more difficulty learning, but we had an easier time forgetting—so we weren't too bothered in the long run.
2. A perceived purpose improves the morale of the learner. Thousands of GI's have had experiences in which they've had to "hurry up and wait," in which they've moved from place to place under the most adverse circumstances, and in which they could see little if any purpose to the activity. The American ingenuity of the GI was demonstrated when he compensated for this "meaninglessness" by developing the fine art of "griping." So masterful did he become with the "gripe" that he could even see humor in the situation and in his own attitude toward the predicament. The gripe was a compensating factor to offset the meaninglessness of his experience and to maintain his morale.
3. When the purpose is made clear, it gives the learner an opportunity to make intelligent suggestions. He can contribute to the improvement of curriculum, for he may know what meets his needs most successfully. Such feedback is necessary if the learning design is to be most effective. This opportunity for the student to contribute ideas to the learning experience is in harmony with the points of view stated earlier. The curriculum is not formulated and planned by the teacher alone; nor is it to be directed by the whims or moods of the inexperienced learner. The ideas of both are incorporated. When this principle is coupled with the other sources for curriculum development (the nature of the subject and the philosophy of the society), the direction of the curriculum—and more specifically the individual learning experience—is assured of a large degree of validity. In fact, the student's chance to add his ideas tends to increase the validity of the learning experience.

A **third** carefully measured step is that of introducing the students to the fact that there exists (at least in an embryonic stage) a fascinating new formula for education. This new formula is a design in which the students may travel as fast and as far as their inquiring minds may take them. It permits them to move in the direction of their interests. It may add to their personal responsibility as learners, but this has not been an objectionable feature to life as most students see it. It reveals to them that their educational progress is due largely to their personal sense of responsibility; hence, within a short while their motivation becomes basically intrinsic.

Boredom is the plague of youthful minds in the relatively unchallenging environment of the traditional classroom. The existence of boredom is a startling reality; in it we see appalling disinterest in that which is the very essence of humanity: the opportunity to use the mind for creative purposes. If the activities of the mind do not challenge us, what makes us different from the cattle of the field or the dog lying beside the rocker?

The learner, at present, does not have fascinating opportunities to pursue individual interests—and his interest fades into boredom. Add to this the realization that this sameness will continue for nine months a year for a paralyzing number of years, and the student will create his own world to protect himself from the prevailing boredom. In the new formula, however, there are several opportunities for fascination—the student is not tied to a deadening schedule, he is not sentenced to nine months of a particular activity. Further, he has a considerable degree of choice in his learning experience while moving toward those objectives basic to his success. To add to this advantage, the student may accelerate both in the subject areas of his intense interest and in those areas in which he is somewhat disinterested but in which he desires to reach a certain level of competence in order to develop a tool for advancing in more important areas of his academic pursuits.

At this point some may question the practicality of this claim. "Do you mean to say you're attempting to take all the work out of learning?" Not really, but we are saying that there is work that is drudgery and there is work that is plain, unadulterated drudgery. The eight-hour shift each day is a sentence; quitting time constitutes a reprieve and the worker punches the time clock with a vengeance. The worker spends the weekend forgetting or "drowning out" the realities of the past week and hiding from the reality of his work life of the coming week.

Happy is the man, on the other hand, who has found his way into a work with which he is physically, mentally, and socially compatible. The same principle holds for the student. If the setting and the learning opportunities can provide a fascinating array of challenges that are not deadened by a rigid time element, a locked-in schedule, and a series of irrelevant requirements, the path of the learner can be a continuous exploration of new frontiers. This concept is far more practical than "starry-eyed." We recognize there are many unexplored frontiers in the academic, scientific, social, philosophical, physical, and spiritual areas of human existence. The bored, time-serving student will not step off his back porch to pursue those untried paths. He is more likely to don the slippers and bathrobe, clutch the cola can, and settle down to broaden his base before that tube that has become a monument to dyspepsia.

The step at which many adults will stumble is the **fourth** one—a step that involves the students in planning, in evaluation procedures, in counsel, and in criticisms.

To bring inexperienced youth into the inner circle of curriculum planning is a procedure not welcomed by many adults. "After all, what do the kids know about what they need? They don't have the experience or years; they haven't yet encountered the hard knocks of reality." And the resentful adult adds, "Besides, we have to take too much from the kids nowadays anyway!" Perhaps all these reactions are sprinkled with a few grains of truth, but they leave a bad taste of distrust that is self-defeating.

No thoughtful educator would leave educational planning entirely to the kids; few would let them flounder in their own sea of uncertainty and confusion. Yet, when youths are involved in curriculum planning, their contributions are often amazingly mature and practical. "Out of the mouths of babes" is not a meaningless, sentimental phrase. One writer well remembers a student-principal council established in a small private high school. The recommendations made by the student group in dealing with educational issues revealed a maturity not expected from the young. Yet, the insightful solutions proposed by the students should not have been a surprise—after all, the students were immersed in the school program. Their direct involvement in the curriculum and their problems within the school structure gave their questions and their proposals a certain relevancy not attainable by those who were on the educational sidelines. It was also heartening to see the integrity of student thought as they recognized the problems and even the dilemma of administrators and teachers. When educators lend an honest ear to the thoughts of students, they can build a loyalty and a dedication to excellence not often seen in these times.

The **fifth** major consideration in preparing students for innovative activity is to incorporate the Five I's of Innovation (see chapter 5). As the Five I's of Innovation are applied to dealings with the community, so, too, should they be applied in dealings with students. In a sense, these I's (Involve, Interact, Inform, Invite, Inquire) are a recapitulation of what we have already said of the innovator's relationship to students, but in a larger sense they say something more. Application of the Five I's implies that we are turning to the students as real persons, important human beings who have our honest consideration. It shows that we view them as present human beings living in the now; we are not merely looking to their future value to the nation, to the community, and to their family.

AS THE TWIG IS BENT

Very likely the botanist studying the growth of plants would give as much study to the tender shoot and the twig as he would to the mature plant. He would give each stage of growth careful study and analysis. If the botanist were to feel that he could learn only from the mature plant, his findings would be questionable. In fact, we cannot imagine a botanist who would refuse to learn from the growing plant and from each stage of its development. The growing plant has much to tell him. The medical doctor must demonstrate the same wisdom. True, he may question a mother about her child's actions, behavior, aches, and pains; but he must also, whenever possible, communicate directly with the child. He has to find out where it hurts, how it hurts, when it is better.

It is our conviction that any innovative program in education that is launched without careful evaluation of the learner's thought, experiences, interests, and needs is doomed to failure. It will have a rocky start and a cataclysmic end. And thus it should be. Such would-be innovators are Culpable Personnel who will experience the Constant Pain of a Consuming Purgatory—and that ain't Continuous Progress, brother.

When the fanfare is over
the curriculum is what happens
when the teacher slams the door and
is face-to-face with students.

MOTIVATING THE MOTIVATORS

7

Let's assume that you are the principal of a high school in a district that is committed to the continuous progress concept of education. If the teaching staff is not also committed to the concept, you have a problem! A very big problem, in fact. For when the chips are down and teachers are face-to-face with students, the teaching process is reduced to a very personal one that intimately involves the teachers' individuality, personality, and most cherished beliefs about what the teaching-learning act should be, as well as about what the teacher-student relationship ought to be. As an administrator or supervisor, you should know that no matter what you may have tried to impose on the teachers' methods or on their beliefs, no change will occur until they have actually internalized the continuous progress concept and have both intellectually and emotionally made a commitment to it.

THE PAINFULNESS OF CHANGE

One wise old superintendent observed, "When the fanfare is all over, and the 'moment of truth' has come, the curriculum **is** what happens when the teacher slams the door and is face-to-face with his students, alone." In such moments, the teacher is going to operate in whatever style he believes in, is comfortable with, and has become accustomed to using. Indeed, he can do nothing else until he has come to believe in the possibility that some other method might be more effective. This is a painful realization for any conscientious teacher; it makes it difficult to escape the conclusion that the teacher, throughout all of his previous career, has been less effective than he might have been. No hard-working teacher will easily accept such a conclusion. After all, the measurement of learning is at best illusory and difficult to accomplish, and almost all teachers can point with pride to many of their students who have succeeded, both academically and occupationally. These are shining examples, indeed, justifications of the teacher's effectiveness. As for all those students who failed to learn—well, everybody knows you can't blame teachers for that! Who would deny that every class has its dull students who cannot learn? Thus armed with objective evidence of the effectiveness of their methods, most teachers have a built-in defense against change.

On the entire educational scene, the toughest person to change is the teacher, because an alteration of methods touches his ego, his self-concept, his security, his life work, and everything that he has become throughout his professional career. An attitude that is brought to a rational level and subjected to analysis is more readily altered by logic. But how can one attack with logic the vague and unexamined belief that is more akin to an emotional commitment than to a product of the intellect?

In view of all this, how can a school principal hope to bring about change, not in just a few teachers, but in an entire school staff? The enormity of the task boggles the mind, yet it is not an impossible one to accomplish; indeed, in many places it has already been done. Let's make some suggestions, both for what to do and for what to avoid.

THE FUTILITY OF FORCE

A principal who contemplates the use of force with a professional staff should avoid getting out of bed! This will have two advantages: It will delight his detractors, who believe he seldom gets out of bed anyway, and it will avoid antagonizing his supporters. In today's climate, when many administrators have to negotiate practically everything but the air they breathe, no principal can afford to antagonize his supporters unnecessarily. We are fifty years beyond the time when classroom teachers were inadequately educated high school graduates who needed the constant directives and ceaseless surveillance of the principal, with his superior education and judgment. Now, the principal, as a generalist, is patently unable to be an expert in all of the diverse areas included in the comprehensive curriculum, and he is keenly aware that in many areas his staff members' expertise exceeds his own. How ill advised he would be to expect to be an effective agent of change on the basis of administrative dicta! A principal just might succeed in coercing a teacher's overt behavior, but there is no way he can coerce the teacher's thinking. And until that teacher actually believes that the continuous progress concept is a better way to go, it will be impossible for him to use the method effectively, even if he is willing to do so in the absence of an intellectual commitment. The main reason we are against coercion is a very pragmatic one—it won't work!

OBJECTORS—CONSCIENTIOUS AND OTHERWISE

By the term conscientious objector, we refer primarily to the teacher who may not know exactly why he opposes the proposed change but nevertheless is convinced that he is against it. We confess to using the term "conscientious" somewhat facetiously in order to differentiate between this position and that of the teacher who has a rational basis for his opposition. A principal can come to grips with the teacher whose opposition is based on a rational objection. Far more difficult is the teacher whose opposition has no solid base. We suspect that the first step in dealing with this kind of teacher is to do whatever seems necessary to bring the teacher to a realization of the actual bases for his opposition. We have already suggested that one of these reasons may be the teacher's belief that his accustomed methods have proved successful, so why change? Or, he may fear failure if he tries the unknown. Whatever the reasons for his position, he must be helped to understand them and to examine the alternative objectively. Once this understanding is accomplished, the principal can work with the teacher with some hope of success.

Next, let's consider the steps that should be taken in preparing the teaching staff to engage in continuous progress education. At this point, we are assuming a staff of teachers who, though not necessarily all enthusiastic adherents of the method, are truly open minded on the subject and willing to examine the concepts without bias.

THOROUGH ORIENTATION

We included a thorough orientation as the first step, even at the risk of stating the obvious—an error we would regard as an egregious insult to the intelligence of our readers. We submit that the need for thorough orientation is not as obvious as it might appear. Consider for a moment the hundreds of years during which many assumptions about teaching and learning have prevailed. If education is not the oldest profession (and we understand that it isn't), it may well be a close second, and it is disquieting to realize how many of its assumptions have remained unchanged through the ages. For instance, far too many teachers, as well as students and parents, still see education as the process of passing information from the teacher to the student, and back to the teacher on demand (i.e., on examination day).

The rigid, lock step organization of education, in which credit is still tied to time, is not exactly extinct yet. Likewise, the A-to-F grading system, even though under assault, is still by far the most prevalent one in use. And we could mention other such assumptions. So, it is not stretching a point too far to say that many of our most time-honored educational practices are so thoroughly imbedded in our bedrock of unquestioned dogmas that it will require intensive and extensive effort to dislodge them. Thus, if one hopes to promote successfully any departure from old methods, one cannot be too careful to orient his teacher-students as painstakingly as possible.

In trying to accomplish this task with groups of teachers, we have repeatedly been struck with our own lack of thoroughness, despite our certain knowledge of the need to be thorough. It is disconcerting to be halfway through the process of explaining the continuous progress concepts to a group of teachers only to be interrupted by someone with a question that shows you he got lost way back at the beginning! It's almost like delivering a lecture on the combustion engine only to discover that some of one's students are not acquainted with the wheel. In orienting a traditionally trained faculty to continuous progress concepts, once-over-lightly will not get the job done. Our advice to the principal is to be as meticulous as one knows how to be and to take nothing for granted. Even very intelligent people need careful explanation and illustration of new and complex concepts.

HEY, MR. PRINCIPAL, TAKE IT EASY!

The natural tendency for a change-oriented principal is to acquaint his staff as quickly as possible with the concepts of continuous progress education and then attempt to go directly into the action phase of implementation. Very apropos here is the lament, "The hurrier I go, the behinder I get!"

Unless his is a most unusual situation, a principal is unlikely to make eager beavers of all staff members merely by going through the process of explaining the concepts to them. Initially, teachers may fall into three categories. Without doubt, some will be downright hostile to the whole idea. Others may be open minded but beset by reservations. A few may be easily convinced and eager to push ahead. But it is a safe bet that at first there will be no unanimity among the staff, and to attempt to push ahead without it will jeopardize the whole operation.

What should the principal do? We've already said it: Don't rush. It is usually wise to allow plenty of time between the point of commitment to change and the actual implementation of change. Three years, in many cases, is not too long to allow for the many things that have to happen before one can successfully launch a new program. First of all, let's consider the problem of the teachers who are unequivocally opposed to change. If the principal pushes them into involvement in a teaching method they oppose, they have two obvious options. They can resort to open rebellion, or they may give lip service to the idea but perform in a manner deliberately designed to scuttle the administrator's best-laid plans. Either alternative is unacceptable.

Here it must be mentioned that for some teachers, because of their age, type of experience, and personality, a major change in teaching methods is not only objectionable, but impossible. A teacher who is opposed to the continuous progress concept on philosophical or any other grounds is incapable of functioning within the framework, meeting the demands, or developing the skills required by the program. For such people, the threat of the unknown is more than they can cope with. If the district has allowed three years for preparing to implement the program, the principal can inform teachers of this fact and urge those who prefer not to participate to request transfer to some other school in the system. Administrators should avoid the conclusion that any teacher who opposes the proposed changes is doing so because of animosity toward the principal or because of some other unworthy motive. It is far likelier that the opposition is based on other factors.

Whatever a teacher's motives, if he is strongly opposed to the program, it is only fair to give him adequate time to seek a situation where he can continue to find fulfillment and satisfaction in his work. In one district, the target date for implementation was set for five years after the decision to change. During that time, satisfactory arrangements were made for all teachers, and only those who were eager to be in the program were involved. Such periods may not be required in all districts, but districts where they are not necessary are the exception rather than the rule.

Teachers in the remaining two categories usually need only time and involvement in the planning in order to become successful participants in the new program.

GETTING WITH IT

Staff involvement is necessary first of all to do the gargantuan job of remaking a grade-oriented, time-bound curriculum into a program that is organized into levels through which the student can move at his own pace. Staff involvement is also necessary as an educational process, to prepare the staff to teach in this mode and to understand the concept at a practical level. A traditional teacher, suddenly transferred to an operational continuous progress program, would be unable to function in this system. It is the process of organizing subject matter into levels, and all the philosophical and organizational changes that accompany this process, that prepares the teacher to function effectively as a facilitator of learning in the new program.

The process that a staff goes through in order to reorganize the curriculum for continuous progress is unique to each school or district in which the process occurs. Obviously, it would be foolhardy to yield to the temptation to generalize and to state unequivocally that specific sequential steps must be taken in all cases. Usually, however, as a staff organizes itself to accomplish the job, tasks often occur in a somewhat regular order, which we will now describe.

Before the actual curriculum reorganization begins, staff members will often visit innovative schools with functioning continuous progress programs. In the case of larger schools, it is usually not possible for an entire staff to engage in this visitation. Staffs usually organize themselves into committees along departmental lines as a convenience in doing the curriculum work within the various disciplines. All or part of a department group may participate in a school visitation, depending on the size of the group and other local factors.

Some committees may wish to have certain research projects carried out before making final decisions about impending curriculum changes. Such assignments may be made on the basis of the abilities and interests of particular committee members. Arrangements are made by mutual agreement of committee members. Members work at tasks that they feel are important and that they are interested in. Often, with each department constituting a committee under the leadership of a chairman (who may or may not be the regular department chairman), the process of curriculum reorganization proceeds at an astonishingly good pace. It must be recognized that there is a need for overall coordination in this process. Occasionally, the schedules or activities of certain committees may conflict, or other situations may arise that will require either mediation on the part of the leader or, on occasion, an outright administrative decision. Naturally, this is the function of the principal. Ideally, such impasses are few, but when they occur, all parties have to know where the buck stops. An internecine conflict between two committee chairmen may do more damage in a short while than can be overcome in many months. Such frustrations of effective group process cannot be permitted to deter the whole program.

In his role of facilitator and coordinator of the committees, the principal, as usual, is seeking a delicate balance. He attempts to function as one among equals, yet there is the inescapable knowledge on the part of all that if authority is required in order to get the job done, the principal has it. However, it is most unfortunate if the principal has to rely on his status authority rather than on the authority of earned respect of the group in order to resolve conflicts.

After desired school visitations have taken place, necessary research projects have been completed, and specific near- and long-range plans have been agreed upon, committees are usually ready to get down to the long and arduous task of breaking loose from grade-level and textbook bonds and organizing curriculum content into levels. (The specifics of these tasks are dealt with elsewhere in this book and need not be repeated here.)

All of the foregoing will be taken, we hope, to convey our

conviction that complete involvement of the staff is an absolute necessity in order to prepare properly to embark on a program of continuous progress education. The process of preparation is itself enabling. It is of utmost importance and should be allowed whatever length of time seems necessary, as long as there is evidence that the staff is proceeding with all due speed and that no one is deliberately attempting to delay the process.

WANTED: DO-IT-YOURSELF SKILL BUILDERS

If there is a moment of truth in the process of the staff's preparation to teach by the continuous progress method, surely it must be the point at which every teacher must develop certain new skills. We do not mean, however, that the teacher must master new or revolutionary techniques of teacher-student interaction. That moment when something the teacher says or does impinges on the student's thinking and causes learning to occur is a highly personal interaction and is so subtle a function of the teacher's total self that it is hardly subject to third-person modification. Perhaps it would be more precise to say that new organizational skills must be developed. Teachers who are either timorous or skeptical should take heart. Continuous progress education does not involve total retraining. It requires only a new way of organizing content and a new way of thinking about student success and failure. There are only three basic organizational skills that must be learned.

First, the teacher must learn to **identify major concepts and subconcepts as components of curriculum units.** This skill is at the heart of the whole continuous progress concept and is an essential part of the process of removing curriculum content from its grade-level, textbook, time-bound orientation. What we are saying is that it is necessary to look at a given discipline in its entirety and to organize it in terms of its major concepts and related subconcepts, removing all grade-level boundaries. The end product will be the same range of content divided into levels or units rather than into grade levels or semesters. These units give structure to the learning task. They are the steps in the ladder, if you please, that lead from the simplest concept at the lowest level to the most sophisticated concept at the highest level. Mastery of each of this series of concepts is the key to progress. Therefore, the proper sequencing of concepts is the **sine qua non** of the entire process. Organizing the curriculum content in conceptual terms has already been dealt with and will not be repeated here. Our purpose here is to emphasize the absolute necessity of teachers developing this fundamental skill.

Second, the teacher must learn how to **write behavioral objectives.** Later, we shall explain (probably in more detail than some of you care about) the rationale for and the technique of writing learning objectives in behavioral terms. Our purpose here is to stress the point that this skill is absolutely essential for the teacher. It is the mode of operation day in and day out, and the teacher who has convinced himself that he cannot write behavioral objectives or teach in behavioral terms will be nonfunctional in a continuous progress program. It might be disquieting, but not amiss, to observe that in this era of accountability, nonfunctional teachers are not greatly in demand.

On a more positive note, we should point out that in writing objectives, as with any skill, speed and ease come with practice. What seems time consuming and onerous at first later comes to seem a natural way to think and write after the teacher has indeed developed skill in the process. There will come a time when the teacher almost automatically thinks in behavioral terms. Then the writing of behavioral objectives will be no more time consuming than it now is for a teacher to put any of his instructional plans into writing. Our plea here is for the teacher who is still ill at ease with writing objectives not to reject the technique in the mistaken belief that it is an unbearable burden. If the teacher will simply be patient during the early phase of objective writing, he will one day discover that he is doing it more easily and quickly than he would have imagined possible.

We do not for a minute deny that writing behavioral objectives for all of one's instructional plans seems at first an overwhelming burden, but we would point out that there is another, easily avoidable, problem that should be considered. Some teachers increase their burden unnecessarily by writing objectives that are not essential to the mastery of the concepts being taught. The teacher must develop skill in identifying essential objectives and in distinguishing between these and nonessential objectives. Every objective should be subjected to the scrutiny of the question: Is this objective essential to the mastery or clarification of the concept? If the answer is negative, the objective need not be written.

Finally, care should be taken to write objectives at all levels of the cognitive domain. We have found that almost without exception, teachers just beginning to write objectives do so primarily at the first two levels of the taxonomy, knowledge and comprehension. We have noted elsewhere that this results in objectives that are criticized as trivial and without cognitive strength. No one would denigrate objectives written at the basic levels. Without them there would be no possibility of functioning at the higher levels. But unless thought is given to the matter, there is great danger of falling into the habit of writing objectives at these levels only. After all, the excitement and challenge of intellectual effort occur primarily at the higher levels of abstraction. To neglect these more sophisticated levels is to miss most of the fun of the teaching-learning interaction.

Third, the teacher must learn to **develop learning activity packages** (LAPs), or their equivalent. There are numerous continuous progress programs operating successfully in which LAPs are not used—at least not under that specific terminology. It is, obviously, quite acceptable to organize the curriculum content into levels or units consisting of behavioral objectives that specify with considerable precision what the student is expected to do. The main danger is that of organizing units too large, so that too much time is required for completion. The student loses motivation when working on units so large that he rarely completes one. One way to avoid this problem is obvious: Write shorter units! Another way is to use the LAP as the basic unit. Obviously, it is also possible to write LAPs that are too long, but for some inexplicable reason it seems that the LAP lends itself to a smaller amount of content than do levels or units.

A well-written LAP contains six rather distinct parts. Not being given to nit-picking, we will not quibble should one choose to include something else in one's LAP, but we think these six components are essential:

1. State, explain, and illustrate the primary and secondary ideas or concepts that are essential to the LAP. If these concepts are dependent on a somewhat obscure or unusual rationale, this should be dealt with as an integral part of the explanation of the concepts. Nothing else in the LAP can possibly succeed if the student starts out with an unclear idea of the concepts to be mastered.

2. Administer a pretest to determine the student's entry level of knowledge. It is fundamental to the whole concept that a student should work at, and not below, the level of his present knowledge. Pretests for each succeeding LAP should be given until it is determined which LAP constitutes knowledge the student does not already have.

3. State each learning objective in behavioral terms, including any explanation or clarification that might be needed. Care should be taken to state the objectives so explicitly, and with such precision, that the average student can understand what behavior is expected of him from a careful reading of the objective and without teacher explanation.

4. Design a listing of learning activities to facilitate achieving the objectives. Important here is the inclusion of optional activities, all of which lead to achieving the objectives of the LAP. If concepts of individualization are meaningful at all, we must recognize the necessity of providing different learning routes to the same objective. In constructing a series of LAPs, care must be taken to prevent the student from consistently choosing options that enable him to avoid using any underdeveloped skills he may have. This tendency is only natural, and LAPs should be constructed so as to prevent this practice.

5. Include in each LAP activity options that go beyond those

essential to the minimal achievement of the objectives. We have chosen to call these quest activities. They are activities designed to give more penetrating or sophisticated insights than the average student will gain from the LAP. It seems likely that these activities will almost necessarily involve the student's functioning at such levels of the taxonomy as analysis, synthesis, judgment, and evaluation.

6. Administer a post-test. In a sense, this test evaluates not only the learning but also the teaching. Given the student's intelligence and application, if he did not learn what was taught, it was not taught—at least not to him! This leads us to reiterate that unachieved objectives indicate inadequate or incomplete instruction. There is unfinished business to be conducted before the student has completed that LAP.

If you keep these six components in mind as you write LAPs, we predict that you will soon come to appreciate and use skillfully the instructional advantages of this learning tool.

OTHER CONSIDERATIONS

One should not confuse teaching style with methods of organizing curriculum content. We have already alluded to the fact that one's teaching style is highly personal and unique and is not in any way hampered by the continuous progress method of teaching, whether or not it involves LAPs, units, or levels. Just as a LAP includes alternate activities to help students achieve objectives, there is room for an infinite number of personal teaching styles that can be used to help students achieve objectives. To assume that traditional, textbook, grade-level oriented methods of teaching provide more latitude for diverse styles of teaching strikes us as an unsupportable and somewhat humorous assumption. The old lecture, read-the-text, take notes, and repeat-on-the-examination mode of education, still so common, seems a poor vehicle to be defended on the grounds of providing opportunity for a variety of teaching styles. Organizing curriculum content in behavioral terms in no way constricts one's style of interaction with students.

We have said much, elsewhere in this book, about the importance of evaluation. If a student's progress from one level to the next is dependent upon his achievement of objectives, it must be perfectly clear to him that his own failure to achieve objectives is the only factor that can prevent him from advancing to the next level. Often the student's self-evaluation will make it clear to him that he still has unachieved objectives to master. This must be made clear not only to the student but also to his parents and to anyone else directly concerned either with the student or with the instructional process.

Finally, we strongly recommend that the reader take pains to differentiate between the open-school concept and that of continuous progress education. The two are sometimes confused in the minds of teachers as well as parents. The open-school concept is far less structured than what we are proposing in the continuous progress program. In some cases, the open school has almost no structure to its program. There may be conditions under which this type of organization is advantageous, but we are not recommending it as a method of instruction to be used for most students. This is not to be construed as an indictment of freedom for students. We have made a case all along for individualization of instruction to accommodate individuals' unique needs. But we are of the opinion that maximal learning occurs when there is freedom within a well-understood structure, so that consistent student application to the tasks of learning is not totally dependent upon the whims of the student. It would be naive not to recognize that, even under the best of circumstances, learning is not always fun and games. There are many times when it is just plain hard work, and at such trying times, most students need the security of established structure and requirements.

Principals will be increasingly
at the eye of the educational storm and
are therefore the most appropriate
group to be concerned with instructional
leadership.

LOOK WHO'S LEADING NOW

8

School principals are functioning at the end of one era and the beginning of another. Ending, or ended, is the era when the principal could devote himself exclusively to the managerial, housekeeping functions of running a school. Very much with us is the era that demands that the principal be the instructional leader of his school. (We are aware of at least one recent article in the literature that takes the position that the principal need not be the instructional leader, but this voice is so overwhelmed by the majority that we are not impressed with it.) If you are a principal and this state of affairs bothers you, bear in mind that this era is not going to go away. So plan accordingly.

Principals will be increasingly at the eye of the educational storm, and are, therefore, the most appropriate group to be concerned with instructional leadership. We have been told for so long that the teacher is the most important person in any school that even some principals have come to believe it! There is, of course, a sense in which this is true. But there is another, broader sense in which this statement is utter nonsense. For better or worse, the principal influences the total school—faculty and students—as no one else can. In terms of both the quantitative and qualitative aspects of his influence, nobody in the school is more important than the principal. He can create a climate that is either conducive to learning and open to innovation, or one that is hostile to both learning and innovation.

If the implication of the title of this chapter is not clear, let us make it so. The title implies that if the principal is not the instructional leader of his school, such leadership will emerge from within the faculty. But it is not enough to acknowledge this, for it does not take into account the following four factors:

1. Informal leadership that emerges within the faculty is multidirectional and results in a loss of both unity and faculty movement toward group goals.
2. Informal leaders have no authority to speak for the faculty, the administration, or any other segment of the school.
3. When problems occur in the innovative process, teachers have no security or official support when their leadership is informal.
4. Research shows no instance in which curriculum innovation has succeeded in a school without the understanding, support, and active leadership of the principal. The principal's active involvement at a developmental level in the innovation is required.

THE PRINCIPAL'S ROLE

We are saying unequivocally that the principal's leadership is essential in implementing innovative curriculum programs. Why is this? There are at least four answers to this question. You might express them differently, but in our view, the reasons are these:

1. Working in the area of the untried always generates insecurities—on the part of parents, the public in general, the board, and especially the faculty, who are the primary "doers" of the innovation. Dealing with these insecurities requires repeated information and explanation with one consistent, supportive, authoritative voice. It cannot be left up to each teacher to explain the program as he sees it. (Some teachers can't "see it" for sour apples!)
2. The principal is a highly visible status figure in the school environment. There is a myth among faculty that the principal is so busy he only has time to work on important matters. Hence, when the principal gets actively involved in instructional innovation, he is telling the faculty that instruction is of primary importance in his hierarchy of values. Principals usually verbalize this message but kill it by their daily priorities. The rather frequently observed practice of assigning one administrator as assistant principal in charge of instruction downgrades the importance of instruction, because the practice is usually interpreted as evidence that an assistant can devote his time to instruction but the principal cannot. We are of the opinion that the principal should retain instructional matters to himself.

3. When the principal is involved in instructional innovation and other curriculum concerns, it gives the teacher assurance that if there are setbacks and problems in the program, the principal will understand the problem and will be supportive.
4. Innovative programs must be evaluated, and the principal has no basis for such evaluation if he has not been involved in the program.

In the past, what passed for evaluation was actually just teacher-rating for purposes of recommending retention, transfer, or separation. This kind of "evaluation" has nothing to do with determining whether or not learning objectives have been achieved. The procedures of the past are inadequate for today. Evaluation must relate to instructional objectives. Obviously, if the principal does not have firsthand knowledge of the instructional objectives, he is in no position to attempt to determine whether they have been achieved. Current legislation in most states mandates some means of establishing accountability for everyone involved in the process of education. Such legislation makes it impossible for the principal to remain remote from curriculum innovations or other more routine instructional concerns.

WHAT ARE THE BEHAVIORS EDUCATIONAL LEADERS NEED MOST?

1. The leader must be aware of the hidden sources of power. Power, which exists in both formal and informal groups, is defined as "the ability to move people." Effective leadership is often dependent on a knowledge of the informal power structures in social groups, in the community, and within the faculty. The intelligent leader knows that power individuals must be consulted and does all he can to enlist the cooperation of these individuals. By so doing, he enhances the chances of his group reaching its desired objectives.
2. The leader must be an effective listener. This task is difficult because a principal is used to being listened to! Role reversal is not easy. Some psychologists say that listening deflates the ego and lessens the self-concept, which is why people vie with one another for attention. It should also be remembered that what a teacher verbalizes to the administrator does not necessarily reflect his actual thinking. The administrator must listen carefully enough to perceive the teacher's actual meaning.
3. The leader must respond to feeling. It sometimes takes considerable sensitivity to discern what an individual is feeling instead of what he is saying. Unless, of course, he is the parent of a child the principal has disciplined—in which case, the principal may not have much difficulty in discovering what the parent is feeling!

4. The leader must remember that people act in terms of what they believe. Administrative edict will never move faculty members toward innovative teaching. Until teachers believe in the new concepts, a new program will go nowhere. The administrator, at any level, who hopes to change faculty behavior by edict, betrays either an overoptimistic view of his effectiveness or an inadequate perception of human nature. Until teachers believe in the worth of a new concept or method, nobody has enough authority to force them to implement that concept or method and to make it succeed. This would seem so obvious as to not need stating, but some administrators have tried the edict approach to innovation, to their sorrow and frustration.
5. The leader must stimulate and direct change. Change can only be accomplished in an atmosphere in which teachers are convinced that they can try something and fail without being punished. The principal must be willing and able to stand up against critics. Much patient explanation may often be necessary, but the ignorance of a few vocal people should not frighten the principal into retreating into the security of the traditional simply because everybody's comfortable with it.
6. The leader must himself be secure enough to deal with the untried. He will seldom have any guarantees that a given method is going to work. He must be willing to take the risk, and to start all over if necessary, without constantly looking over his shoulder or worrying about every wisp of criticism that blows across the campus.
7. The leader must share authority with teachers in order to get the job done. One research study has shown that in any educational program, teacher participation is twice as high when the principal shares authority rather than exerting it in the traditional unilateral manner.
8. The leader's behavior should ensure that in all interactions each staff member will, in the light of his background, values, and expectations, view his function as one that builds and maintains his sense of personal worth and importance.
9. Although the principal shares authority with teachers, he still retains his leadership role, functions, and responsibility. At the same time, his leadership activity is guided by an increasing interest in developing individuals who are fully functioning, productive, and self-responsible.
10. The leader's central thrust must be toward encouraging the competence of teaching, compelling those within his sphere to search beyond the traditional for new truths, as well as leading the way toward a constant reappraisal of techniques.
11. The leader, as an **instructional** leader, must make a major commitment of time and must be willing to cultivate new skills. He must be willing to put instructional leadership at the top of

his agenda and keep it there. It may well be that the demands of educational leadership in the future will require a restructuring of the principalship and its demands. What has been good enough in the past is not necessarily acceptable for the future. If the principal can't do everything, then he must establish his priorities and delegate those tasks that are of secondary importance to second-level building administrators. We have already expressed our view that the principal should not delegate instructional leadership to subordinates.

It is one thing to know what one is supposed to do and quite another thing to put it into practice. The situation is like that of an old farmer in a southern county. The local agricultural adviser was trying hard to persuade him to try a new method of raising cotton. Finally, in desperation, the expert said to the old farmer, "Man, you don't seem very much interested in improving your farming." To which the old man replied, "Young fella, when it comes to farming, I already know better than I do."

The administrator has the complicated task of adapting the schedule and the school plant to meet curriculum needs.

The administrator must reshape the school to fit ——— the curriculum.

ON THE LEVEL AND UNDER WAY (CURRICULUM)

9

All talk and mere theory can tire the best of minds. It's logical now to ask the question, "Just how do you organize the curriculum in order to implement a continuous progress education for each learner?"

In putting forth an answer to that question, we would warn against two conclusions. First, no one should conclude that we think the following procedure for organizing the curriculum constitutes the only method of proceeding. As educators, we need to recognize differences in schools, in communities, in students, in subject areas, and among teachers. These differences certainly affect the organization of the curriculum and the procedures to be followed. Second, we must warn against oversimplification. Hence, in the following recommended procedures we must be aware of the many ramifications that need to be given consideration as one actually gets down to the implementation of a program.

Nevertheless, regardless of cautions, we need to strike out on a path toward the curriculum organization that is basic to continuous progress education.

WE LOOK AT STRUCTURE

Any worthwhile building has been started with a plan; the foundation has been laid, the framework has gone up, and it has been completed with those furnishings that satisfy the needs, purposes, and aesthetic sense of its occupants or users.

Continuous progress education has at its foundation the needs of the students and the goals of the society that it serves. To fulfill these needs and purposes, we must establish a framework upon which they can be built. Jerome Bruner has been credited with setting forth the concept of "structure" in education, and as a starting point we will use his approach to look at the major discipline areas or subject areas taught in schools.

First, we look at a particular discipline—math, for example. We ask, "What is the structure of this discipline along which the student is to progress?" Or, we might ask, "How can we organize this discipline from K through 12?"

To answer these questions intelligently, we need to look at just a few terms. The first term is "structure" itself. It may be defined as a body of knowledge so organized that it can be most readily grasped by the learner. As Bruner states, "The merit of a structure depends upon its power for simplifying information, for generating new propositions, and for increasing the manipulability of a body of knowledge. Structure must always be related to the status and gifts of the learner" (Bruner, **Toward a Theory of Instruction,** p. 41).

Bruner next introduces us to "sequence": "Instruction consists of leading the learner through a sequence of statements and re-statements of a problem or body of knowledge that increase the learner's ability to grasp, transform, and transfer what he is learning. In short, the sequence in which a learner encounters materials within a domain of knowledge affects the difficulty he will have in achieving mastery" (**Toward a Theory of Instruction,** p. 49).

He states further, "There is no unique sequence for all learners, and the optimum in any particular case will depend upon a variety of factors, including past learning, stage of development, nature of the material, and individual differences."

Next is "scope." Scope is "the range within which an activity displays itself" **(Webster's New Collegiate Dictionary).** It may be viewed as the span or range over which the learning opportunities extend in a particular discipline.

Another term, one that is not satisfactory to all educators, is "level." A level constitutes a major concept within the structure. Or, it may comprise a family or cluster of concepts that need to be mastered before a learner steps up to the next level within the discipline.

Having defined sequence, scope, and level, we are now in a position to structure the discipline. The scope takes in that structure from bottom to top. The subject area is divided into levels—logical concept areas that need to be mastered before moving on to the next group of concepts. These levels are placed in sequence, from the simple to the more complex. The learner moves up this academic ladder as he demonstrates his competence through his performance. (This is where the behavioral objective fits into the pattern.)

When we look at the structure of a discipline, we are looking at the whole package.

For example:

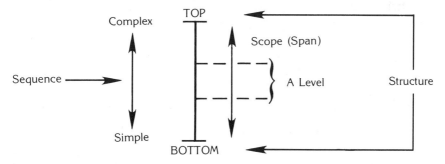

WE NEXT EXAMINE THE LEVEL

The number of levels within the structure of a discipline may vary according to the nature of the discipline. For example, math may have more levels within its structure than does communication arts. If we remember that a level represents a learning task dealing with a major concept (or skill or family of concepts), it could follow quite logically that some concepts may take longer to master than others. Thus, in some disciplines the concepts may involve a greater time span before mastery is attained.

Having viewed an example of the structure of a discipline, we should now isolate a level from the structure and examine it closely.

We see, **first,** that a level deals with a major learning concept. Let us suppose that this level deals with the ability of the learner to multiply mixed fractions and whole numbers.

Second, to determine readiness for this level a preassessment needs to be made. This preassessment might be in the form of a pretest. Obviously, the pretest must measure the student's ability, or lack of ability, in multiplying mixed fractions. The preassessment may not be limited to a written pretest; it might include some other procedures, such as an interview, oral questions, and so forth. In any case, the preassessment must be accurate to insure the proper placement of the learner. Diagnosis is synonymous with preassessment in this setting. This step is basic to individualized instruction and to the larger concept of continuous progress education. Real progress for the learner cannot take place unless we find the level of competence at which he can function or at which he is ready to function. It is at the preassessment stage that traditional education has been at fault. We have needed to develop a bureau of misplaced learners, because many students have been placed in inappropriate learning situations.

Third, objectives must be written to give direction to the learning opportunities within the level. These objectives may be set up as recommended earlier. The major concept may be written in the form of a general instructional objective (see Gronlund, **Stating Behavioral Objectives for Classroom Instruction**), or it may be viewed as a goal to attain at the end of the learning opportunities. Then appropriate, measurable behavioral (performance) objectives must be written. These objectives, appropriately written, will enable the instructor to measure the student's progress toward the goal or general objective.

Fourth, appropriate learning opportunities need to be developed for each learner. Individualized learning should be built into each level. The chance to opt or select from a variety of learning opportunities gives the learner greater interest, an increased confidence, and an inner motivation—all of which enhance his chances for success. However, this effort to individualize does not necessitate thirty different options for thirty students. The effort to obtain an absolute one-to-one ratio is unrealistic. Students with similar interests and attainment may be clustered; such clusters come under the classification of individualized instruction.

Fifth, self-testing opportunities should be set up for students. The learner should be able to measure his progress through available quizzes or testing devices. This feedback is essential; it gives the student a valid view of education. He doesn't feel the pressure to cheat; on the contrary, he sees the need to understand a concept before he can move on to more complex concepts.

Closely related to the student's self-testing is the principle of a continuing evaluation or feedback. Too often education has consisted of final exams, unit exams, or midterm exams. This end-of-the-line type of measurement does not lend itself to aiding the learning process; it merely indicates the results. In an athletic event the coach or manager and the participants keep a careful eye on the progress of the game. They make adjustments and changes to meet the requirements necessary for success. Similar processes, or "game plans," are used in business, war, love, or any other serious endeavor. Certainly the same careful analysis must be made of the educational progress of the learner.

As the student gets older (high school or college level), he needs less frequent assistance in the periodic, ongoing sampling of his progress. But in any learning situation the learner must be aware of growth and progress.

Sixth, teacher-made tests must be developed that accurately determine the student's performance and readiness to advance to the next level. These tests should relate directly to the objectives set up for that level. They should measure what the objectives seek to attain. The established criteria should be high enough to insure mastery of the concept dealt with in the level.

"Mastery" is an elusive term. Just what constitutes mastery? In this case mastery may be viewed as "minimal mastery." We must ask, "What is the minimal performance necessary for achieving success at the next level?" For some students this may be all that can be expected. For more gifted students, the mastery level requirement could be much higher for moving to the next level of study. (If this were not required, the program would promote the slipshod learning that is so prevalent today.)

Throughout the student's experience at a particular level, there should be sufficient opportunity for appropriate practice and for interaction with the instructor and other students.

The score on the teacher-made test (or post-test) should not reflect a lucky bit of guesswork in which the student is able to cool the test. It should be evident that the student has attained a level of competence that reflects his readiness to move on. Regardless of the form the teacher-made test may take, it should show that the student has clearly reached the objectives.

At various levels throughout the scope of the discipline, certain standardized tests might be administered. Used correctly, these tests might reveal the need for certain adjustments in the local educational program. On the other hand, the local program must not be governed by national norms. A number of factors must be brought into focus. The educator may find that mean scores (arithmetic average) for the local community should be considerably higher than the national norm; or, the reverse may be true. The dangers inherent in the use or misuse of national norms should be recognized by the educator, the parent, and the student.

"Enrichment" is a word that has become rather unpopular with a large segment of parents and students. It conveys to these folks the concept of busywork. And that is often the case. Better students are often given large numbers of problems to work because they have the ability to do so. This misuse of enrichment is seen by many parents and students as a very unsatisfactory practice. Such a stance by the teacher is not justified. It is not true that the better student needs more practice than does the slower student. But this is what takes place in such a so-called enrichment program.

There is, however, a valid view of enrichment. If we think of the structure of a discipline as a skeleton, then we can readily see that a student should have opportunity throughout his learning experience to put flesh on the bones and to breathe a living experience into the body. Having a gifted student go dashing from one level to another merely putting the bones together is as extreme a position as giving him a large amount of repetitious busywork. It may readily be seen that neither point of view is acceptable. Admittedly, a balance is difficult to achieve. Any educational program that merely supplies enrichment opportunities cannot be viewed as actual continuous progress education. On the other hand, a continuous progress education program that does not provide for enrichment may actually be building a misconception of what education involves into the student's thinking. In the initial implementation of a continuous progress program, the student may desire to take off and move readily from one level to another. The teacher, in his corresponding enthusiasm, may be very happy for this evident motivation. However, if the student is encouraged merely to put together a skeleton, the whole educational program may come back to haunt the teacher and the student.

A CONCERTED CURRICULUM

The administrator has the complicated task of adapting the schedule and the school plant to meet curriculum needs. He needs to reshape the school to fit the curriculum. This reshaping may involve clever adaptation of old buildings. The Scriptures indicate that one should not put new wine into old bottles, but the same injunction should not be applied to putting a new curriculum into old buildings.

The administrator's task also involves the reshaping of the time concepts in the schedule. If he cannot break up the inflexible fifty-minute-period five-days-per-week schedule, it is unlikely that he will be able to establish a curriculum fitted to the individual needs of the learner.

In the final analysis, effective curriculum organization involves the concerted efforts of administrators and staff members. It necessitates the most efficient approach to the use of buildings, space, and time. It means structuring each discipline to allow for the continuous progress of individual students. It requires a common philosophy in which there is general agreement on the concept of individualization. It searches for the best means of utilizing the professional staff and other nonprofessional personnel. It calls for careful recording of progress and for those evaluative procedures that measure the growth of individual students.

The issue is paradoxical: It is, on the one hand, an overwhelming task; and yet, its simple philosophy presents a fascinating challenge to the innovative educator.

If we, as adults, were to experience continuous failure at our work, we would do something about it.
We would not tolerate an atmosphere of failure to envelope us.

A MAJOR TOOL OR A MISERABLE OBSTACLE? 10

The educator who would meet the challenge of accountability today must give serious consideration to the behavioral objective. This consideration is important whether the educator desires to stay within a traditional mode of education or whether he desires to pursue some innovative endeavor.

The demand for accountability, although harsh in its sound and overtones, is a legitimate demand. It implies a series of questions: Is my child learning? Is he learning what he ought to learn? Is he learning all that he ought to in the time involved? How much is it costing? Could more learning take place with less cost? Are the teachers teaching the right values, or is there some Communist plot insidiously insinuating itself upon my American child? The questions may go from the reasonable to the wild; but the educator who is prepared for the challenge of accountability can meet these questions with equanimity.

It is our assertion that the behavioral objective is not only a major tool in meeting the challenge of accountability but also a basic instrument in the administrator's planning—in giving direction to his task, in measuring pupil progress, in meeting individual needs, in bringing personal satisfaction to his life as an educator, in designing appropriate learning experiences for individual students, and in recognizing strengths and weaknesses in the curriculum.

THE BEHAVIORAL OBJECTIVE EXAMINED

If, then, the behavioral objective is so fundamental a tool, just what is it? How does it differ from objectives as we have known them in other contexts?

Any competent educator or thinker in other vocational pursuits has had goals and objectives toward which he has worked. In education, a goal is thought of as a general accomplishment toward which the educator strives. It is not specifically detailed and is often thought of as timeless. For example, a teacher-training institution may have as its goal the development of competent young teachers. The goal doesn't speak of the specific characteristics that may be required to develop competent teachers. These detailed, specific characteristics are identified in the objectives. The goal may be viewed as the ultimate accomplishment at the top of the ladder; the objectives, in this illustration, would be the rungs of the ladder that lead toward the goal at the top. It is generally understood that the learner climbs these rungs step by step. The teacher-training institution would have a series of objectives that would lead to the development of competent teachers. Among these might be skills in various teaching methods, class control, communication, testing, and evaluation of student progress, and basic ability in guidance and counseling. As the prospective teacher climbs these rungs, reaching these objectives, he gets closer to the goal of becoming a proficient teacher. (The illustration is oversimplified, of course, for we recognize that competency in teaching is not a static condition but a continual growth experience.)

Now, the behavioral objective is different in that it places emphasis on what the learner will do as a result of a certain learning opportunity. For example: "The learner will type." If we were to say, "The teacher will teach the learner how to type," we would not have stated a behavioral objective (unless we were measuring teacher competence). The behavioral objective stipulates what the learner will do.

Having said, "The learner will type," we have stated our objective in behavioral terms, but we have not yet stated it well. There are four basic factors that are essential to the composition of a good behavioral objective (see Mager, **Preparing Instructional Objectives**). These factors are such integral parts of an objective that they take very little memorizing. The simple package is made up of four components.

First is the learner—we are interested in what the learner will be able to do as a result of certain learning opportunities.

Second is the verb—the verb must denote observable, measurable behavior on the part of the learner. Here an explanation is in order. The verb "to know" does not meet the requirement for a behavioral objective. The objective, "The student will know arithmetic," does not make a clear statement by which one might measure performance. The statement could imply simply that arithmetic is a subject area with which the student has some acquaintance. On the other hand, it could imply that he is very skilled in arithmetic. In either case, there is a large measure of uncertainty as to what is expected of the student and as to what his actual skills are. In the behavioral objective much more specificity is required. Verbs are selected that will help us view the learning experience with much greater accuracy: "The student will be able to add whole numbers," "He will be able to multiply mixed fractions," "He will identify the basic procedures for changing fractions to decimals," and so forth.

The **third** component of the behavioral objective is the condition under which the student is able to demonstrate his learning competence. The condition might be a ten-minute test (a condition too often used perhaps). It might be a situation in which the student must determine the board feet needed for a bookcase. Or, it might be a setting in which the student needs to double a recipe in a cooking class. The conditions under which learning may take place are countless.

Fourth, a complete behavioral objective, one that will identify measurable outcomes in the learner's experience, must have a criterion, or standard that establishes the expected or required level of performance.

Now let us complete our earlier objective, "The student will type." This initial statement contains two of the four basic elements: first, the learner or student; second, the verb, "will type." The verb denotes a definite, expected behavior. Now we add the third element, the condition: "In a ten-minute test the student will type." As stated earlier, the student performance will take place under the specific condition—a ten-minute timed test. The criterion, standard, or performance level completes the behavioral objective: "In a ten-minute test the student will type at the rate of thirty words per minute." The standard, obviously, is "thirty words per minute."

It may be appropriate to have more than one criterion in a behavioral objective. In our example, it is very logical to have an additional criterion: "In a ten-minute test the student will type at the rate of thirty words per minute with no more than five errors." Here the proficiencies expected in the criteria are both speed and accuracy.

The football fan may look at the four parts of the behavioral objective much as he would the four members of a backfield (perhaps in the old T formation):

	(2) Learner
(1) Verb	(3) Condition
	(4) Criterion

All four are essential to the success of the team. If any ground is to be gained, all four must function together. The illustration may be carried a couple of steps further. First, the teacher, whose role might be equated with the coach, is the designer of the learning opportunity. He sets up the plays. True, he may consult his players in certain situations, but essentially it is the teacher's task to design learning opportunities and to design them in such a way as to make successful performance possible or even probable.

Second, the learner is the one who must carry the ball. This principle is sound scholastically and athletically. Regardless of the brilliance of the coach, if his players can't or won't execute the plays, there will be very little success. In the same sense, the use of the behavioral objective places an appropriate share in the responsibility of learning on the learner himself. It is not only the teacher (or coach) who must be accountable—the student shares in this responsibility.

Even today there are students who will take the ball and run with it; but there are others who spend their time kicking the educational ball or, even worse, punching holes in it.

FACING OBJECTIONS

Let's look at some of the immediate objections to the objective.

First objection: You sure picked an easy illustration. Anyone could write an objective for that learning experience.

Response: Very true; we picked an easy illustration. But this was for the purpose of clarity. If we were to stay at this level in writing objectives, the criticism would be valid. Furthermore, this is why the behavioral objective is currently under so much criticism. Too many educators are writing objectives solely at this intellectual level. In following the line of least resistance, educators write a host of objectives that do not make sufficient demands on the learner or the instructor. In a sense, the objectives themselves may not be wrong, but the writer has omitted the more demanding levels of thought. Basically, what we are saying in our response is that the behavioral objective is not at fault; the fault is in the failure to utilize this tool in its deeper dimensions.

Second Objection: The use of behavioral objectives results in experiences similar to training in animals, not in true education.

Response: Admittedly, if the objective continues to be written at the lowest level of the intellectual ladder, the result is mere training. We can train porpoises to leap through hoops; dogs to sit up, roll over, and bark; horses to count via hoof beats; and kids to do comparable things. Once again, the responsibility lies with the educator to ascend the educational ladder in selecting or composing objectives to challenge the learner. It should also be noted that a large number of the learning opportunities set forth by educators who do not employ the behavioral objective may also come under the classification of mere training. (We will deal later with objectives eliciting higher intellectual responses.)

Third Objection: The writing of behavioral objectives is too time consuming; in fact, to the busy teacher, it is a waste of valuable time.

Response: The writing of valid behavioral objectives does take time. But once the objectives are written (and, of course, well written), the teaching-learning opportunities take on more meaning, a sense of direction is recognized, purpose becomes clear, evaluation becomes more accurate and effective, and student-teacher relationships become more amiable (for student and teacher are now working together toward reaching the same basic objectives). These assertions will become more evident as we proceed further into the investigation of the behavioral objective as a tool.

When the task of composing behavioral objectives is not fully understood, it becomes too time consuming. Two authorities help us overcome this hurdle.

Norman E. Gronlund suggests that the educator write certain general instructional objectives that deal with basic concepts or principles within a discipline, subject, or unit. These general objectives are not measurable or behavioral as such. (Some writers would refer to these as goals.) But these general instructional objectives deal with important major concepts that are basic to the student's success in the course or particular discipline area. These objectives employ such verbs as "understand," "comprehend," or possibly "master." For example, a general instructional objective might be stated as: "The student will understand the symbols employed in the unit on electricity."

Under such a general objective (in which a major concept is to be mastered), Gronlund suggests writing just enough behavioral objectives to accomplish the mastery required in the general instructional objective. In this case, the behavioral objectives may be along the following lines:

1. The student will be able to define, in his own terms (without necessarily memorizing), each symbol employed in the unit.
2. The student will employ these symbols correctly in applying them to the solution of a basic problem.
3. The student will recognize correct and incorrect applications or usages of these symbols in the context of the study of electricity.

(In these behavioral objectives, for the sake of brevity, we have not included all four factors of a behavioral objective as emphasized earlier.)

Gronlund gives the following illustration of the relationship of behavioral objectives to general instructional objectives:

"Uses critical thinking skills in reading. (General)

1. Distinguishes between facts and opinions. (Behavioral)
2. Distinguishes between facts and inferences.
3. Identifies cause-effect relations.
4. Identifies errors in reasoning.
5. Distinguishes between relevant and irrelevant arguments.
6. Distinguishes between warranted and unwarranted generalizations.
7. Formulates valid conclusions from written material.
8. Specifies assumptions needed to make conclusions true."

If we were to follow Gronlund's scheme a step further, we might view the developing course or unit through the following scheme:

I. Goal (general)
   A. General instructional objective (important major concept or idea, but not immediately measurable)
      1. **Behavioral objective** (specific, measurable)
      2. **Behavioral objective** (specific, measurable)
      3. **Behavioral objective** (specific, measurable)
   B. General instructional objective (major concept)
      1. **Behavioral objective** (specific, measurable)
      2. **Behavioral objective** (specific, measurable)
      3. **Behavioral objective** (specific, measurable)

The number of general instructional objectives needed, or for that matter, the number of appropriate behavioral objectives, is determined by the nature of the subject, the needs of the learner, and the thinking of the society in which the school is functioning.

The experienced educator can readily see that this schema avoids the need of writing countless behavioral objectives for each course—the number of which could become a compendium as thick as a Sears catalogue.

Another educator who helps us boil down the number of objectives to a realistic, workable level is W. James Popham. He not only relieves us of this insurmountable burden but also helps us develop a better behavioral objective. He does so by showing us a principle to avoid while giving us a principle to adopt.

He suggests, first, that many writers of objectives have mistakenly written test items rather than acceptable behavioral objectives. Such an objective might read, "The student will be able to work correctly nine of the ten multiplication problems on page 23 of the text," or, "The student will be able to solve all of the odd-numbered problems on page 67."

With such an approach, the teacher would have to write an objective for every problem or item that the student should be able to work. The task would be endless. Early proponents of objectives found themselves in this dilemma; furthermore, diligent teachers who have worked in this direction have become discouraged with objectives and the insurmountable task of developing them. An additional problem is the student's reaction. If the objective states that the learner should solve the odd-numbered problems, the learner can object vigorously when given the even-numbered problems to work. (The reader may object to this simple, negative logic, but the experienced teacher has often heard the inane objection, "You didn't say we had to solve the even-numbered problems!")

Popham's sensible approach helps us to avoid both the endless task of writing objectives and the negative reactions of students and educators to the test-item approach. This is accomplished through incorporating the concept that Popham calls "content generality" into the task of writing behavioral objectives. In contrast to the test-item objective, the behavioral objective containing content generality measures student competence in dealing with a major concept or with major factors within a major concept.

Thus, a behavioral objective that is written with the concept of content generality in mind might read, "Given any set of twenty multiplication problems involving numbers of three or four digits, the student will be able to solve 90 percent of the problems correctly."

The test-item type of objective involves the student's ability to solve a particular list of problems. His ability to solve that given list may be indicative of his ability to solve multiplication problems in general; but, on the other hand, he may originally have had some assistance in working those problems and may have subsequently (at least in part) memorized the answers and even the steps leading to the answers. He may become upset and do very poorly with a different set of problems of comparable difficulty.

With the objective containing content generality, the student definitely needs to know how to solve multiplication problems at the level stipulated. There is little or no opportunity to memorize or to come up with the right answer without knowing the principles of multiplication. To meet the requirements of such a behavioral objective, the student must understand the principles of multiplication and must demonstrate his proficiency. When he does, one can draw the conclusion that the student knows how to multiply.

Test item objectives are easy to write but hard to swallow. The teacher may boast of being a tough teacher by writing: "The student will be able to name the first ten presidents of the United States," or, "The student will be able to name all the presidents of the United States," or, "The student will be able to name all the Democratic presidents of the United States," or, "The student will be able to list the battles of the Civil War, who won, and who the generals were on each side."

The victim (student) becomes irritated, exasperated, and discouraged by the meaningless, almost endless chore of memorizing facts.

For these reasons, the teacher should write behavioral objectives that involve content generality based on meaningful learning experiences.

Thus, if the educator adopts the principles for writing objectives introduced by Gronlund (the general instructional objective and its related behavioral objectives) and by Popham (objectives incorporating the principle of content generality), he will overcome the objections that writing objectives is a waste of valuable time.

Most remaining objections to the behavioral objective will be answered as we consider other facets of the behavioral objective and as we recognize more fully the role of the behavioral objective as it relates to education in general. However, there is one other objection to which we should give attention: the objection of those who view the behavioral objective as a tool of the behavioristic psychologists.

Behaviorism suggests that human beings are not basically free—that, in fact, freedom isn't the issue in life. It suggests that people can be programmed much as a computer is programmed— that through a stimulus-response type of conditioning, a person's behavior can be shaped. (B. F. Skinner is perhaps the leading proponent of modern behaviorism; see his works, such as **Walden Two** and **Beyond Freedom and Dignity**). To the individual who thinks of freedom as a condition of paramount importance, behaviorism presents a dismal view of life. The behavioral objective is identified by many as an outgrowth of behaviorism. In reality, the similarity in the two terms is an unfortunate coincidence. Admittedly, the behaviorist would very likely adopt the behavioral objective approach to learning, but the proper use of behavioral objectives does not lead to the adoption of the behaviorist psychology of education.

Because of this unfortunate similarity of terms, many educators have renamed the behavioral objective. "Performance related objectives," "instructional objectives," and "performance criteria," are a few of the terms adopted to avoid the objectionable implications.

Now, the behavioral objective neither forces upon the educator a restrictive philosophy of education nor puts the teacher into the mold of one style of methodology or teaching procedure. The objective and the teaching method are not to be viewed as identical. Two excellent teachers could have nearly identical objectives for their particular course and yet each adopt a style of setting up learning opportunities that is quite different.

A defensive, apologetic approach to a subject is often self-defeating, so we will not linger longer on the topic. It is essential, however, that we should recognize the nature of the opposition and the purported weaknesses of the behavioral objective.

A TOOL FOR HIGHER-LEVEL THINKING

An immediate appraisal of the behavioral objective leads many to conclude that the behavioral objective supports a product-oriented education—that is, that it is concerned merely with the outcome, or getting the right answer. It seems to encourage the mere learning of facts, coming up with the answer, or giving back to the teacher that which the teacher has dispensed the day before.

The process-oriented educator is often opposed to the behavioral objective concept. The process-oriented teacher is interested in developing in his students the ability to think for themselves. He wants the student to discover, to solve problems, and to reflect. He feels that the process of learning how to learn is more important than learning the facts themselves. The students may not know the answers, but they know how to go about finding the answers. They know the processes through which they might come up with the product, should that product be of sufficient value to merit the research. Such learners are not encumbered with a host of meaningless or unusable facts, but they can pursue that which is meaningful and relevant to their needs and to the needs of society.

But the beauty of the behavioral objective is the fact that it is **not** limited to product-oriented education. This approach can also be used to develop in the student the ability to learn how to learn. When the educator writes objectives eliciting higher levels of thought, he encourages the development of the ability to go through the intellectual processes of learning—he encourages the learner to learn how to learn.

At this point we might well take a look at what Bloom and his committee have done in their **Taxonomy of Educational Objectives: The Cognitive Domain.** A first look at the **Taxonomy** may elicit a ho-hum response from many: "After all, that stuff looks too dry and technical." But a closer view reveals that Bloom's committee has done careful work in developing a system of classification of the different levels of learning. The basic outline touches on six major levels of the intellect. From the lowest to the highest levels it encompasses knowledge, comprehension, application, analysis, synthesis, and evaluation.

Much as a biologist classifies a grasshopper or a frog, Bloom and his committee have classified the different aspects or levels of the intellect. They have taken each of these aspects and have identified subclassifications. However, the educator does not have to become a scientist to use these classifications. With a little study, he can recognize the various areas of the intellect (called the cognitive domain) and can write objectives that elicit the kind of intellectual behavior specified.

In other words, the educator need not stay at the lowest level of the educational ladder in preparing objectives. He need not limit his objectives to such requirements as: "The student will list the first ten presidents of the United States," or, "The student will memorize the Preamble to the U.S. Constitution." Rather, he will be able to write objectives at more demanding cognitive levels, such as: "In studying the presidential campaign of 1948, the student will identify those factors that led to Truman's reelection" (analysis), or, "Given a map of a currently uninhabited region, the student will select the most appropriate location for a city" (analysis, synthesis, and evaluation).

The point here is that the educator who uses these objectives can place his emphasis on the process of education as well as on the product. He need not look only for answers; he can examine the student's ability to follow appropriate educational processes.

In fact, we believe that the educator who takes time to set up appropriate objectives will more likely help his students to develop the ability to discover and solve problems than will the educator who ignores these levels of the taxonomy. Many a teacher has thought he was cultivating the thinking power of his students while, in reality, his students were confused as to what the teacher really wanted—they were merely searching for the answers that would satisfy him and assure their getting a decent grade. Such a learning experience does not represent the true process of learning.

Perhaps a balance should be maintained in education—a balance between product and process. Certainly there are facts that need to be learned; there are answers that need to be given. These are products. Unfortunately, however, this is where most education bogs down. We should move beyond products to the realm of ideas, to the great issues, to discovery, and to reflection on the meaning of things. This aspect, the process, has too long been neglected.

THE TOOL IN PERSPECTIVE

The use of the behavioral objective can enhance the program of traditional education, but in continuous progress education it becomes an integral part of the curriculum. A brief review of the elements of continuous progress education will help us recognize this assertion.

Continuous progress education is an endeavor to fulfill the educational goals of society and to meet the individual needs of the students. In the process of helping society with its goals and its educational objectives, the behavioral objective becomes a recognizable tool. The society, in setting up its goals, needs objectives of a specific nature to determine whether or not these goals are attainable and to assure that the educational system is moving in the direction of those goals.

If the student is ever to experience continuous progress in his education, there is much that educators need to know and to do. They need to know what the student's current abilities are. They need to know the level at which he is currently functioning academically.

They must ascertain his interests and needs. They must measure his growth.

If we were to switch to medical terminology for a moment, we would say that a diagnosis of the student must be done. This step is logically followed by a prescription—a prescribed course of activity to help him overcome his deficiencies and to help his growth experiences. Medical tests are given to patients for a variety of reasons, but here we would do better to return to educational jargon. Education speaks in terms of evaluation, and this is fundamental to progress.

Evaluation takes place in every aspect of education:
1. It takes place when the society sets up its goals and objectives.
2. It takes place in the diagnosing of student needs. This preassessment needs to be accurate and concise.
3. It comes into focus in setting up the learning opportunities for the student.
4. During the student's course work, while he is going through certain learning experiences, feedback (or evaluation) is essential for measuring growth, and it is essential to know that the student is growing in the direction of the basic goals.
5. At the "end of the line," evaluation is again required. This evaluation touches not only the student but many other people and factors in the educational system. Did the student grow sufficiently and appropriately? Was the teacher effective in contributing to this growth? Did board and administrators provide the framework and structure needed? Did society bear its responsibility and were its goals realistic? Was the curriculum adequate for the needs of the student and the community?

We hope our point has become apparent by now. Too often society in general and educators in particular are far too vague in assessing the task of education and in evaluating education's accomplishments. Now, the simple behavioral objective pulls us all down out of the ethereal clouds of education and insists that we face the realities of life. Not satisfied with the uncertainties of vague platitudes and praises, it insists on our looking at actual outcomes. It helps us diagnose and prescribe. If we err in these tasks, we adjust. But we know that adjustment is necessary when the behavioral objective is employed. We can see when objectives are beyond the ken of some learners, and we can see when students are already proficient in the areas of the objectives that have been set up. In either case we redo—we reset the requirements to meet the needs, interests, and goals of the student and society.

During the learning experience, feedback, or ongoing evaluation, takes place. When this feedback is placed alongside the behavioral objective, our evaluation of student progress can be quite accurate. In such a setting, both the student and the teacher view evaluation as a natural experience measuring progress. Both the student and the teacher are looking for growth; both share responsibilities in that growth. The antagonism between student and teacher is unnecessary; the fear of exams and tests is alleviated; there is no longer the student's feeling of being tricked by the teacher's sneaky questions. Progress toward the goals becomes the predominant theme of both learner and teacher; they share accountability for reaching the goals.

A THING OF BEAUTY?

Calling a behavioral objective a thing of beauty may bring forth a derisive laugh from veteran educators. The writers have obviously "flipped their lids." How can a tool, even if it is practical, be referred to as a thing of beauty? Basically, the beauty of the objective is in the direction that it gives to education, in the way it meets so many needs, and in its preventive ability—its tendency to keep serious educational problems from developing. More specifically, the beauty of the behavioral objective is witnessed in:

1. Its **flexibility.** The objective is not rigid. It can be written at different intellectual levels; it enables the teacher to give individual attention to students; and it allows the teacher to choose from a variety of styles or methods, picking one that he prefers or that he finds most applicable to the learning setting. It frees the teacher and schedule from the need for the rigid five-day-per-week schedule of classes. Time, place, and number of students may vary without fear of confusion or loss of valuable learning opportunities. Not only does the behavioral objective permit flexibility, but it reveals the need for adaptability and change to meet the varying circumstances.
2. Its **unobstructiveness.** It does not stand in the way of change. The teacher is not handcuffed by the objective—he is freed. He knows that any legitimate educational method is encouraged, as long as the objectives are approached and ultimately reached.
3. Its **accountability.** If accountability asks, "What are you doing?" the objective provides the answer. If it asks, "Where are you going?" the objective makes it perfectly clear. No single tool meets the demands of accountability more directly than does the well-written behavioral objective.
4. Its **healing qualities.** Here we beg for a bit of literary license. You may ask, "What did an objective ever heal?" Well, a serious and unfortunate situation has developed in most educational circles. Unfortunate attitudinal wounds

have scarred the relationships between students and teachers. Many students have felt that teachers enjoy deceiving them. The teacher is often viewed as one who accentuates his own brilliance by revealing to the students how much they have missed or failed to accomplish on an exam. (In some cases, unfortunately, this **is** an accurate assessment of the teacher's position.) Evaluation, or the testing game, becomes a contest between students and teacher. It isn't uncommon for students to get together to help each other search for what might be asked on the test. The purpose of the test seems almost to be a secret withheld from the student. The establishment of objectives does away with this "war and games" approach to learning. Teacher and students get together, the objectives are clear to all, the teacher's task is to aid the student in his move toward the objectives, and the evaluation (or test) is for the purpose of determining the degree of mastery of the objectives. In such a setting, with such a task, the teacher can be just as disappointed as the student when the objective is not reached. He searches for those methods, or those learning opportunities, that will accomplish the task. With such an attitude toward his role, the teacher finds that the barrier between him and the student has disappeared. The teacher no longer takes pride in his "toughness," but in his ability in helping the student succeed.

5. Its **humaneness.** This whole approach to establishing the value of the behavioral objective may appear to be one soaked in a gushing sentimentality. Before that conclusion is drawn, however, let us recall that a large segment of students, from elementary school through high school, are choked much of the time in a smoggy climate of failure. The D's and C minuses are multiplied (the F's are cut down in a mild effort to be kind—or to pass the student on to someone else); these low grades are recorded; observations are added; and the reputation begins to build: This is a poor student. This procedure is repeated year after year, and it takes extraordinary courage on the part of a teacher to give a good grade to the student who has the reputation of being a slow learner.

If we, as adults, were to experience continuous failure at our work, day after day, or month after month, we would do something about it. We'd quit (or get fired). In any case, we would not tolerate an atmosphere of failure to envelope us. Yet we wonder why certain students get negative—why these students bide their time until they can drop out of school. We wonder why they select friends with similar experiences. They must succeed in something, and they succeed with one another. When these students get home, they are again immersed in the awareness of failure—their parents remind them of it. And the old man is ready to remind his kid of how successful **he** was when he was a kid—if not in school, at least when he went to work at the age of eight.

There is a certain cruelty in the process of labeling a student a failure or a poor student and then following it up by wave after wave of negative reinforcers—contrasting our successes with their shortcomings.

If any educator, or any parent for that matter, should reject the important principle of humaneness in education, he should really review his purpose in pursuing his vocation. If his primary concern is his subject area, his personal academic ego, his upward mobility on the social scale, or his financial security, he is in the wrong occupation. The student will recognize this fact, and the teacher will be a detriment to the educational processes. On the other hand, if a teacher has a real concern for the needs and individuality of young human beings, he possesses an attribute that will move him in the direction of pedagogic success and fulfillment. And what could be more rewarding than to guide a youthful member of society into a climate radiating with prospects for success, to assist him in the development of those tools that will enable him to keep on growing toward his full potential, and to catch his look of appreciation—even though it be just a fleeting, furtive glance in one's direction?

If a beginning pitcher were required to grip the ball in the same manner as the veteran... he might never become a competent performer.

LEARNING IS THE NAME OF THE GAME (METHODOLOGY)

11

No sports writer would dare refer to a pitcher merely as a "good" pitcher or a "great" pitcher. If the pitcher is a left-hander, he becomes a "stylish southpaw," or if he has a generous waistline from living the good life, he may be known as the "portly portsider." The sports writer searches for those word pictures that will capture the imagination of his reading public; so he writes not only of the stylish southpaw but also turns his attention to the "brilliant rookie" and to the "fireballing right-hander who can really bring it."

Through the descriptions of the sports scribe, the avid sports fan is able to follow the career of his baseball idol, from the player's days as a rookie to the shattering experience of being given his unconditional release. When the young fireballing right-hander eventually loses his speed, he adjusts and becomes the "cagey veteran" with the "assorted stuff." He is eventually described as the "sore-armed hurler" who struggles to hang on—to remain a part of the organization. He is finally cut adrift to become a free agent. His career sputters for a few months, until he finally fades into the subculture of work.

The sports writer can help create the legend; he can provide the fanciful imagery with which to inject the hooked fan. But a basic, hard reality surfaces: The name of the game is winning. The writer may contribute the descriptions; the pitcher may toy with forms of delivery; the manager may describe what might have happened if the ball had taken a certain bounce or philosophize by describing baseball as a game of inches; but rationalization doesn't change the grim reality. If the pitcher doesn't win, he's not crafty; if he loses, he is not stylish; and the fan quickly labels him a bum! The latter appellation is readily heard and understood by the owner.

THROWING A CURVE AT THE CURRICULUM

Educators have gotten by much longer riding on the crest of fanciful descriptions. But **accountability** has thrust itself into the center of the morass of educational jargon. The innovative techniques, the amassed maze of media materials, the costly retrieval systems, the cleverly shaped buildings, the journalistic praises—all these must be set aside when we take a look at the real issue: The name of the game in education is learning.

The task of the teacher in many ways parallels the experience of the baseball pitcher. The essential in baseball (that is, to the serious professional) is winning. It makes very little difference how stylish or cagey the pitcher may be. If he goes on losing, he will not last in the big leagues. The essential in education is learning. It's amazing how this fact is so readily overlooked!

Often the young teacher just out of college comes armed with the confidence that he can accomplish what the veteran could not do. This youthful pedagogue is dressed in the mod manner, adopts a grooming more in harmony with the youthful dry look than with the look of the establishment, and is current in his use of the verbal and nonverbal communication tools of the day. Yet with all this, he falls into the same trap as did his predecessors. He has placed himself front and center; his emphasis is on the clever, on the relevant; his attention is on the role of the teacher and not on the central concern, which is learning.

Serious writers remind us of the need to take a careful look at education and its priorities. C. P. Snow suggests that "changes in education will not, by themselves, solve our problems; but without those changes we shan't even realize what the problems are" (**The Two Cultures and a Second Look,** pp. 99–100). He further suggests that the changed emphasis will not only help us to recognize our responsibilities but will also make it difficult to deny those responsibilities. In view of the teacher's responsibility to bring learning opportunities to the student, it is nothing short of appalling to witness the self-satisfaction in the teacher who is classified merely as a brain, as a joker, or as a good guy who doesn't require too much busywork. Whenever the emphasis is on the clever characteristics of the instructor, the central task of learning is in danger of being thrust aside.

C. S. Lewis describes how one comes to an appreciation of art: "We must begin by laying aside as completely as we can all our own preconceptions, interests, and associations ... We sit down before the picture in order to have something done to it, not that we may do things with it. The first demand any work of any art makes upon us is surrender. Look. Listen. Receive. Get yourself out of the way" (**An Experiment in Criticism,** p. 19).

Lewis is not speaking of education directly, but teaching is an art, and the best counsel to be given any prospective teacher is Lewis's "Look. Listen. Receive. Get yourself out of the way." For the name of the game is learning.

We will make no attempt here to tout one method of teaching as better than all other methods; however, we do prefer one central thrust over all others, and we prefer the methods that fit best into this thrust above those that do not.

ELEMENTS OF THE CENTRAL THRUST

How can the teacher provide the best learning opportunities for the student without placing undue emphasis on his own skills, techniques, knowledge, and expertise? He does so by identifying and employing certain basic principles. These principles are concerned with the individual learner and with the continuous progress open to that learner. They constitute a cycle made up of three major aspects: preassessment, prescription, and evaluation.

Preassessment

Preassessment is also referred to as "diagnosis" or "pretesting." The last term is too narrow. Preassessment is actually a combination of formal and informal endeavors to locate the academic status of the learner. It identifies the most logical starting point from which to design learning opportunities for a particular student. Preassessment certainly involves pretesting, but it is more than that. The pretest might be a teacher-made test, a standardized test, or a combination of tests. In addition to the tests, preassessment may involve interviews with students, parents, and other teachers. It is an attempt to get a comprehensive view of the student so that the starting point of his learning experience may be appropriate to his level of functioning.

Preassessment incorporates the concept of readiness, and this readiness of the student brings with it the probability of success in subsequent learning opportunities. It is precisely at this point that conventional education has experienced failure. There has been, too often, a failure to preassess the learner to see whether he is ready for the learning tasks assigned to him. Furthermore, even where preassessments have been made educators have failed to capitalize on the findings of the preassessment—students having wide variations in ability have been given identical learning assignments. Thus, the value of the preassessment is ignored.

We see but little objection to the term "diagnosis" (in place of "preassessment"), but it may imply a sickness rather than a more positive, global view of learning. Whether called diagnosis or preassessment, this initial task of the teacher starts the student on the road to learning. Perhaps educators should be happy for synonymous terms and should avoid insisting on an exclusive, key word for each function or task. Educators are somewhat guilty of succumbing to the paralysis of analysis cited by a noted preacher.

Prescription

The second aspect in the learning cycle is currently referred to as "prescription." Having discovered the student's needs and interests, the instructor prescribes those learning opportunities that relate directly to the preassessment findings. Although one particular technique need not be promoted over another, once again certain principles need to be recognized and employed. The prescription for learning contains the following elements:

1. Clearly stated objectives. These objectives should be within reach of the learner and should lead him in the direction of the goals of the discipline. We don't need to repeat the observations made earlier about the effectiveness of this tool, except to state that the objective should be clear and easily identifiable to the student.

2. Perceived purpose. The reason for the prescription—the purpose in undertaking the learning task—should be as clear to the learner as it is to the instructor. This is the target of motivation. At this point, the student moves from extrinsic motivation, in which the stoking of the fires is done from outside, to the highly desired intrinsic motivation, in which the spark, the ensuing flame, and the steady glow of enthusiasm come from within the learner. An understanding of the purpose for the learning experience may not immediately bring with it the intrinsic desire to learn, but, on the other hand, that desire will never occur if the student perceives no meaningful purpose. The fact that potentially brilliant students often are listed among the nonachievers and the disinterested reveals that little has been accomplished in making clear to them the purpose of the particular learning assignment. If he cannot perceive a meaningful purpose, the learner sees little to justify his staying with the course. Whenever a student questions the value of a certain course, he gains precious little from that course.

3. Active response. This facet of learning is a vital part of the learning climate. If the student must agree with an authoritative teacher, the learning climate becomes oppres-

sive. The student, with his silence, takes his attitude toward the subject underground. The teacher can't know what the student's learning experience is like when he has not permitted open, objective, active responses to the academic setting. The teacher must establish a learning environment, a climate, that encourages active responses to the intellectual stimuli. The responses may agree or disagree with the instructor's position; in every situation the responses should represent the honest point of view of the learner. In no way should this honesty be suppressed.

4. Appropriate practice. This is an ingredient essential to any effective learning design. This principle points up another weakness that prevails in the more conventional or traditional classrooms. The skilled lecturer may be very active, enthusiastic, and knowledgeable, but the greater his skills, the more likely he is to subject the students to a passive, nonparticipative role. Appropriate practice may not be the same for every subject or discipline, but it is essential to the mastery of every discipline. In some subject areas the validity of this principle is so obvious that it needs little supportive evidence. Imagine the auto mechanics class, typing class, or home economics class that does not give the learner opportunity to put the principles studied into practice. The experimentalist is right in his emphasis on learning through experience. The learner does not wait until adulthood before he can put his learning to use—that would be too much like attempting to transport water from the kitchen sink to the bathtub in a sieve—too much is lost in the attempted transfer. "We learn by doing" is more than an old platitude; it is a basic principle of learning. Just a brief caution at this point. Practice must be appropriate—much harm can be done through inappropriate practice. The task of unlearning bad habits is painful, and the practice that is unduly long and wearying is wasteful.

5. Individual differentiation. This is nearly synonymous with individualized instruction. Madeline Hunter suggests that we need to individualize the input-output modality. When we analyze that statement, we discover a concise truth. She is stating that we need to allow each person to learn (input) through those means that are most appropriate to him. By the same token, he is to have the privilege of sharing what he has learned (output) by the use of those tools that he can employ best. If a beginning pitcher were required to grip the ball in the same manner as the veteran, to assume the same stance, to employ an identical delivery, he might never become a competent performer.

On the other hand, if his coach were to recognize his strengths and unique mannerisms and allow him to work from them, the young pitcher would have far greater chance for success. By the same token, we can each recall instances in which we were hesitant to share what we had learned because we were afraid our report might not be couched in the language that would meet the approval of the instructor.

6. Graduated sequence. The learning experience should provide the learner with an opportunity to go from the simple to the more complex; the key to this academic door is the learner's readiness. Permitting the student to move into a situation that is too complex can produce several unfortunate results. One result may be student discouragement. Or, the student may attempt to "bluff his way through"; if he succeeds, he moves into a more difficult predicament, and a vicious cycle develops. When the student attempts to function at a level of complexity for which he is not ready, he also suffers the embarrassment of failure. To avoid such embarrassment, he may resort to devious means of covering his predicament. Among these devious routes may be the practice of cheating; another might be the development of an attitude of hostility. It is difficult to imagine a student cheating when he has the ability to perform the task. It is almost as difficult to conceive of a student's hostility toward a learning assignment that he has the competence to handle. There are those who would argue that some disciplines do not involve a sequence from the simple to the more complex—history, for example. Admittedly, Chapter 25 of a history book may be no more complex than Chapter 2. However, if teachers teach American History at the twelfth year in the same manner and with the same requirements they used in the seventh year, the practice is open to serious question. A graduated sequence can and should be built in the history curriculum. The employment of Bloom's **Taxonomy** can be one means of accomplishing this. The teacher (or curriculum designer) can build the objectives in a sequential manner. That is, he can elicit higher levels of thought as the student progresses through the curriculum. Whereas in his early learning experience the student may have absorbed certain basic historical facts, later he may be expected to analyze the facts of history and finally make evaluative judgments concerning the events.

7. Feedback. All during the learning experience the instructor should be getting feedback to inform him of the learner's

progress. In any journey, the course should be charted and progress should be noted; in most journeys, corrections and adjustments need to be made along the way. The failure to obtain feedback during the learning experience is much like driving a car at night without lights—it is neither safe nor practical, and certainly the sense of direction is lost.

Evaluation

The third aspect in the learning cycle is evaluation. Debates have raged for some time over the practice of issuing letter grades, whether of the traditional A-to-F set or whether some other group of symbols. Each side can present its rationale and defend its position vigorously.

Actually, a gradual change has taken place in grading practices. Some have suggested that the reporting systems have gone through two generations of change. The first-generation change consisted largely of check lists and written observations on the progress of the learner. Second-generation changes have involved either of two major philosophical approaches to education. The proponents of a highly unstructured open concept, or open school, would deemphasize grades and likely settle for a pass-fail type of reporting. Those who advocate a more structured continuous progress curriculum would favor a reporting system that would cite the student's level of attainment; that is, the learner would be reported as functioning at a certain level in each discipline area. The quality of work expected at each level would then be described.

At this point it is not our objective to settle the matter of issuing grades or not issuing grades, of using check lists, or of tossing out grades altogether. We **are** saying that evaluation is a significant aspect of the learning cycle because it is an ongoing task employed to determine the progress of the learner.

Evaluation is more than the third step in a three-step learning cycle; it is a part of the fabric of the first two steps as well. If we were to go back to the preteaching tasks of education—setting up the curriculum, communicating with the community, establishing a philosophy of education, and identifying what is to be taught and learned—evaluation would show up as an essential part of each procedure.

Now let us return to our current objective in this chapter: to identify the components of the learning cycle that has as its major thrust the student and his learning experience, not the teacher and his techniques. As we have seen, the elements of this learning cycle are preassessment, prescription, and evaluation. The cycle might be viewed as a circle of functions moving toward a particular goal of learning:

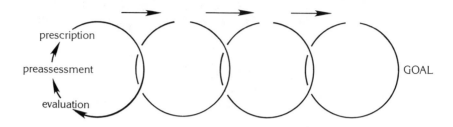

A UNIQUE TECHNIQUE?

A teacher at this point might still feel certain frustrations. Many teachers want someone to "tell it like it is." Just what do you do in the classroom? What visible, workable method do you employ?

As stated earlier, we will not declare one method as being better than another. We will discuss methods only as they relate to teacher-centered or, especially, student-centered concerns. We would not presume to advocate one classroom technique above another as the best for all teachers or all learners.

Teaching methods must allow for the learning cycle that is designed to identify individual readiness, needs, and interests and to allow the student to travel on the learning journey at his own responsible rate. Some methods lend themselves to this design; some do not. In suggesting some methods, we are not declaring them to be suitable for all teachers and for all subjects or disciplines. We are asking teachers to analyze the methods to determine whether or not they allow for individual progress of the learner.

Among the methods that may lend themselves to this approach, none has been cited more often than the learning-package approach. Some refer to these packages as LAPs, or learning activities packages. These packages take different forms and are often developed by the teachers themselves.

For learning activities packages to be developed in a discipline, the subject field must be structured into levels. This might take the form of a comprehensive structure from K through 12, in which case a number of teachers and curriculum specialists might work together; or it could merely involve the structure of the particular course taught by the teacher. The levels constitute major concepts, or families of concepts, that are basic to the progress of the learner through the discipline.

The learning package has as its goal the mastery of the concept involved. The package should include objectives that, when reached, will assure mastery of that concept. The package cites the learning materials and resources to be used; describes the learning experiences and possible alternative experiences to be gained; and outlines the pretests, formative tests (the "in-progress" tests to determine progress toward the goal), and post-tests to be employed.

An error that has occurred among those employing learning packages is the failure to include learning sessions that provide for student-teacher and student-student interaction. Individualized learning, to be most effective, must include certain purposeful large-group experiences, small-group discussions, and individual or small-group directed study.

It should be evident that packages may vary according to the nature of the subject, the interests of the learner, and the talents of the teacher. When mastery of the objectives has been reached, when the criteria have been accomplished, the learner goes on to the next package.

Another caution should be observed: Sufficient time should be given to allow for appropriate practice and to insure thorough learning before the learner exits and goes on to the next level. The time needed for mastery will vary from learner to learner. Quality and careful scholarship should rule over speed.

Variations of the LAPs may come in the form of contracts, both formal and informal. Some teachers may use the chapters of well-constructed textbooks as the levels or packages. As the teacher grows in experience, he adds other resources and gains more and more freedom from the text. The teacher may take old texts that have special chapters of value, cut them up, place the chapters in folders, and use them as levels in the structure.

It is not our intention to exhaust the reader with an extensive list of teaching methods that might fit into the learning design advocated here. However, we recommend that the interested reader look into particular methods, study them in the light of the learning design we have described, and determine personally whether the method could be used, to what extent it could be used, or whether it would find little or no place in the design.

The teacher might start his analysis of teaching methods—whether or not those teaching methods would lend themselves to individualized instruction—by looking first at those methods generally used in conventional or traditional classrooms. In such classrooms, four methods have predominated: lecture, discussion, questioning, and demonstration. Having found or determined the extent to which these approaches might be used in the teaching-learning design, the teacher can next turn to some of the newer, more sophisticated approaches being advocated.

Certain commercially developed simulations and games have found their places in the classroom. The creative teacher might develop his own games. What social studies teacher couldn't make his class into a United States Senate, a judicial courtroom, or a town meeting? Inquiry teaching should also be given careful study. Its concern with problem solving and with the process of learning may provide ideas for individualizing instruction. Inquiry teaching could at least provide the interaction experiences needed in all learning. Programmed learning with all its ramifications may play a significant role in an effective learning design. Here, again, the cost factor may prove discouraging until the teacher realizes that there are many degrees of sophistication in programmed materials. Programming may range from teacher-prepared materials to programmed texts to teaching machines and on up to computer-assisted instruction. Programmed learning is definitely geared to the individual. It would be a mistake to overlook its possibilities.

It would be desirable for each teacher to develop a list of methods. As time permits, he might study those methods as they relate to an individualized learning design. In conjunction with his inquiry, the teacher might visit other teachers in action; from them he can learn, adopt, reject, revise, and adapt.

Schaefer, in his book **The School as a Center of Inquiry,** suggests that the school should provide opportunities for the teacher as well as for the student to create, to solve problems, and to grow. We concur. We believe that in the area of methodology, particularly the methodology that permits individual students to learn and grow at their own rate, the teacher has opportunities to be creative. The teacher certainly has a right to reject proposals that do not appear feasible. The teacher has a right to borrow and adapt from the ideas and practices of others. But the greatest challenge, the greatest delight (or plain fun), can come to the teacher who is willing to think the problem through and who will come up with his own ideas. When he does so, he will find reality in the observation of Kenneth E. Eble, who asserts, "Learning begins in delight and flourishes in wonder" (**A Perfect Education,** p. 3).

We do not condemn the scientist for having failed on a number of occasions... if that scientist eventually comes up with the answers.

TO GRADE OR NOT TO GRADE (EVALUATION)

12

Many irresponsible observations have been made regarding grading, including the suggestion of throwing out grades altogether. On the surface this may seem fair and humane, but it brings up some questions that need to be answered. One is, if you don't employ a grading system, how do you report progress? As a follow-up to that question we would ask, is the reporting and recording of progress important?

One who is opposed to grades might come back with a series of questions: Is a letter grade actually an indication of progress? Do we actually know what a letter grade means? Does the letter grade mean the same thing from teacher to teacher?

THE NEED TO MEASURE

Perhaps we could best deal with this issue by getting to the larger concept of evaluation. We believe we are safe in saying that, regardless of one's position on letter grades or other comparable symbols, there must be a thorough system of evaluation if intelligent directed learning is to take place. A thermometer would be of little value to the physician if the degrees were not marked. A driver of a car would have difficulty knowing the speed he is traveling without a speedometer. We could provide endless illustrations, but we merely wish to make the point that measurement and evaluation of measurement are a basic part of any endeavor in which progress is sought.

As we look back at the various facets of the learning cycle (dealt with in the previous chapter), we find that evaluation is an intrinsic part of every phase. The first phase, preassessment, has evaluation built into it. In the second phase, the prescription of certain learning opportunities for the student is based on the individual needs and interests of the student. This in itself is an evaluation. As we observe the progress of the student on his learning journey, we are again evaluating. Thus we see that evaluation constitutes the very fiber of education and of the learning process.

We would concede that those who are opposed to grading per se have some valid arguments. For example, in traditional education in which a student may have received an F in a course somewhere in his learning experience, that F is placed on his transcript and becomes a permanent record that follows him wherever he goes. This appears to be a situation of double jeopardy. Not only has that person failed, but his failure is brought up again and again wherever that transcript is studied. This is one of the more inhumane aspects of the traditional grading system.

Contrast this with our attitude toward the scientist. We do not condemn the scientist for having failed on a number of occasions, if that scientist eventually comes up with the answer. In fact, just the opposite is the case. He is highly extolled for his brilliance and for his persistence.

We hold the position, therefore, that the traditional system of grading has been inhumane, or at the very least, unfair to the learner. On the other hand, we hold that evaluation is a necessary adjunct to learning. Evaluation should be realistic and it should measure the progress of the learner.

We hold, further, that evaluation should measure the progress of the student against his potential. It should view his progress as the distance he has traveled from a particular starting point.

Some refer to this as "criterion-referenced measurement." In this approach, each student has a real opportunity for success. Few of us are world-record holders in any event, and certainly very few ever become Rhodes scholars. It is unfair to measure us against those who accomplish such feats. When we are evaluated against that which we are capable of doing, however, we have a fair and realistic system of evaluation. Should all students reach an expected criterion, the teacher will need to reevaluate his attitude toward student success. It is not a sign of poor teaching when all students succeed.

We would not throw out altogether what has been called "norm-referenced measurement." Norm-referenced evaluation measures the individual against some norm. It might be the national average, or it may be the average of students at a particular age within the nation, within a state, within a school, or within a class-room. This dimension to evaluation is important because we need to discover, at times, whether our expectations are reasonable and whether the individual will be able to cope with the requirements of society. Overemphasis on norm-referenced evaluation, however, has been very damaging.

When children are taken through eight years of grade school work in which they are subjected to norm-referenced measurement, in which the student is compared with the rest of the class, the children at the lower end of the academic scale eventually draw the conclusion that they are not bright. And the tragedy is compounded when teachers draw the same conclusions. The classification of such a child becomes permanent. A vicious self-fulfilling prophecy develops. Teachers who see the records of these students feel almost compelled to issue the same low grades to these learners. Often, these teachers would be embarrassed if it should be discovered that they have given good grades to those who have characteristically received poor grades from previous teachers. Few of those who evaluate the learners have the courage to adopt the characteristic stance of some popular sportscasters who declare with pride that they "call it like it is."

A PROPOSAL

In view of the existing problems of evaluation we, with a combination of foolhardiness and presumptuous bravado, wish to recommend a set of principles for evaluation. These principles are as follows:

1. Evaluation must take place, and it must measure the progress of the individual. This approach to evaluation is both positive and realistic. It is not a head-in-the-sand approach to failure; for when progress isn't as extensive as it should be, there is a degree of failure. On the other hand, there is no double jeopardy involved, for the very negative F is not on a transcript or on the progress report.

2. The progress measured is based on the principle of criterion-referenced measurement. As stated previously, this approach deals with measurement from two points of view: first, it measures the student against his potential capabilities; then it attempts to help the student realize those capabilities. A reachable standard is set up for the student and his progress is measured by his approach to that standard. When that standard is realized, he is evaluated as having succeeded.

3. We would release the student from a rigid time requirement. If a student, living up to his capabilities, requires six months to attain a certain standard, that student may be evaluated as a success even though another student may

be able to reach the same standard within five months. Obviously, however, if there is evidence that the student is wasting his time, he should be counseled accordingly. It should be clear to us all, however, that we have previously tied ourselves too rigidly to time. There is nothing to indicate that certain materials have to be learned in one semester or two semesters. If it takes a little longer to obtain mastery, these students should be given the time needed. If it takes a little less time, they should be permitted to go on to other challenges.

4. We recommend, since we are dealing with levels within the structure of a discipline, that the report form be one in which the student level of attainment is reported. The report would be meaningless if we were merely to state that he is at Level 36. We suggest, therefore, that a description be given of the performance expected at that particular level. This, of course, would be called a performance-related reporting system.

5. Our fifth principle is that the student should take up his work in a new school year at the level at which he can function. If a student can function at Level 45, for example, he is to start out at that point even though that point may not be the opening chapter of a given textbook. In other words, he may actually start out at what is traditionally the middle of the fourth grade. This principle is obviously basic to continuous progress education.

6. We also recommend that the recording of the student's progress be on the basis of levels and that these levels describe the performance attained or required. From this basic system, the school may set up certain minimal performance requirements for graduation. This would give more meaning to the diploma, for it would be a certificate representing a degree of mastery and actual performance.

7. We recommend the judicious use of norm-referenced achievement type tests. Norm-referenced tests should be given (perhaps once a year) for the purposes of determining the basic abilities of the student and the group, evaluating the expectations of the school program, and providing realistic evaluative criteria for college entrance. In the absence of norm-referenced tests, the school and the teachers in particular might find themselves operating in an increasingly smaller sphere of activities and expectations. The norm-referenced test provides an occasional look across the horizon of education activities to see whether our expectations and our activities are realistic.

8. The end result of this evaluative system is to transfer the emphasis of evaluation from a set of marks (whatever

symbols might be used) to a recognition of performance and ability. Here we reassert the point of our previous chapter: Learning is the name of the game. The evaluative system that we propose provides for learning on the part of all students and for the potential success of all students.

The reporting forms may include other aspects of evaluation that may be considered important. For example, if a school desires to report social habits, personal effort on the part of the student, attendance, and other meaningful aspects of school experience, it certainly may do so. However, at the heart of the reporting system will be the progress of the student in the learning areas undertaken. Because of the large differences in communities and in the interests of people, it would be more than presumptuous to set forth one pupil progress report as ideal for all schools. It might even be desirable to have different pupil progress report forms for the various levels within the school system. We would suggest, however, that basic to any successful reporting system is the matter of clear communications. At certain levels the best communications might come in the form of parent-teacher conferences. Regardless of the level, however, it is certainly self-evident that when communication is not clear, the reporting system will not be effective.

PART THREE

IMPLEMENTATION

Ezekiel not only saw the wheel way up in the middle of the air, he also saw a lot of lifeless bones scattered about.

OUT OF THE DUST

13

Ezekiel not only saw the wheel way up in the middle of the air, he also saw a lot of lifeless bones scattered about. Only when bones are organized and properly articulated can they support a living structure. If we wish to have a viable curriculum, we, too, will need to assemble the bones. We need to identify the parts of the somewhat puzzling task.

In Part II of our foray into the land of innovative education, we were laying out the bones. Lest you are tempted to conclude that this is a dry scene or that it doesn't hold water, keep in mind that bones are blood-producing organs.

SURVEYING THE PARTS

The lifeblood of continuous progress education is in the elements cited in Part II. Let's look at them as a package for a moment.

First, there would be no point to the endeavor if we were not to accept the philosophy that each learner is to be given the opportunity to succeed and to grow in learning as he is able.

Next, the community should accept this philosophy and be prepared for its implementation. In addition, the teaching staff and the students should also accept the philosophy and be prepared for action. It follows that the administrator should know his task and assume the leadership in activating the program.

The disciplines should be carefully structured, the levels and major concepts should be identified, and the objectives should be written. Teaching methods should be employed that are appropriate to each discipline and that lend themselves to individualized instruction. Careful evaluation, reporting, and recording should be instituted to enhance the progress of the learner and to pinpoint the learner's position in each discipline.

If any of these bones should be missing, their absence would pose a threat to any awakening life or to any future life of continuous progress education.

WAYS OF ASSEMBLING THE BONES

Enthusiastic innovators have often attempted to do too much too soon; on the other hand, there are those who would do too little for too long. Just how much, then, should be done at one time? There are various options:

The first option may be made by one teacher within one classroom. This teacher may develop a structure for individualization within one subject area or in several. He may adopt the principles of Part II, allowing each student to progress at his own rate.

One of the problems inherent in this first option is that the learners will likely go back to a conventional program when they move to the next teacher's class the following year. If, on the other hand, the enthusiasm of the first teacher should prove contagious, the next teacher may be inspired to prepare for the same program. In this way the continuous progress concept may spread gradually throughout the school over a number of years.

The second approach involves the cooperative work of a group of teachers in structuring one discipline. For example, the teachers from the first year on, in a cooperative endeavor, may structure a discipline such as math. Incorporating the principles cited previously, they institute continuous progress education in math while teaching the other disciplines in the conventional pattern. With increasing skills and sufficient time for preparation, this group of teachers may expand the continuous progress curriculum outward to encompass other disciplines.

It should be obvious that the third option involves the comprehensive work and cooperation of the entire school. After careful and lengthy study, the administration, staff, and community launch the entire school on a continuous progress curriculum. Many educators are not hesitant to point out that innovations, to succeed, must start small; these educators would likely reject this third option. Yet there is much to be said for "global" planning. A coordinated, cooperative effort provides complete, consistent opportunity for learners at each level.

Of paramount importance in such a move is the acceptance

of the philosophy of continuous progress education on the part of educators, learners, and the community. Haste in inaugurating an innovative plan prior to the acceptance of the philosophy will not only ring the death knell to that particular innovative endeavor, but will very likely kill other ideas that might come up in the future.

Because it is usually very difficult, and in some cases impossible, to get an entire community to accept one philosophy of education, a fourth option might prove the most feasible. This option is the adoption of alternative education. Alternative education takes many forms. A typical example of alternative education, however, may be seen in the Minneapolis School District. Within this district are four alternative schools: a contemporary school, a continuous progress school, an open school, and a free school. Parents and students can select the school that fits their philosophy and their needs. An increasing number of Americans support this education cafeteria in which the learner may select from several options. An advantage to introducing continuous progress education through an approach involving several alternatives is that the learner who becomes disillusioned by one school's approach (or one alternative) may transfer to another school within the system.

ACCORDING TO WHOM?

At this point a "thou shalt not" is that an innovation to be implemented should not reach out to compel those to participate who are not ready or who are not in agreement with the innovation. With this in mind, which of the four options is to be selected by the innovator as the most appropriate way to implement continuous progress education?

The first factor to consider is found within the four options themselves; that is, the method of implementation depends on the size or scope of the innovation to be adopted. Certainly if only one teacher has made adequate preparation for implementing the innovation, the first option (in which a particular teacher introduces the program to the students of his classroom) should be selected. We are not forgetting, however, that the teacher's task includes gaining the cooperation of the administration and preparing the learners and the community. In other words, the scope of the innovation is related to the readiness of teachers, administration, community, and learners.

A second factor to consider in answering the question of which option should be employed in the program's implementation is the philosophical nature of the community. If appropriate communication and study reveal that the community is quite united in its philosophical view of education, any one of the four options might be selected. The actual option selected, of course, would again depend on the degree of readiness of the parties involved. If, however, the community is definitely divided in its philosophical view of education, option three (adoption of a continuous progress curriculum by the entire school) would not be the mode of implementation. In a divided community, the alternatives approach (option four) would be the fairest and potentially the most workable.

A third factor to be held as a guiding principle in any decision to implement a continuous progress program is a principle we will refer to as "localization" (or "delimitation"). Keep the program local; that is, do not permit the implementation of a program to go beyond the current ability or readiness of those who will be affected by the innovation. Exceptions to this principle should be few. A coarser statement of this idea is the old adage, "Don't bite off more than you can chew." Perhaps it should be adjusted to say, "Don't bite off more than you are willing to chew, digest, and assimilate." There are few experiences more distressing than the body's refusal to take the nourishment given; the comparable experience in education is just as distressing.

No one would desire to fly if
he were to suspect that the airline company
had not made adequate preparations
for the entire flight.

PREPARING FOR TAKEOFF

14

Anyone who has experienced air travel, or for that matter anyone who can read a newspaper, knows of the precautions the airlines must take prior to allowing passengers on board. Each passenger is electronically frisked; his luggage is searched; his shaving gear, change of clothes, and business materials are opened to the scrutiny of some grinning young security officer. The more sensitive passenger stands uncomfortably by until the inspection is completed. But the passenger recognizes the need for these precautions and soon forgets the hassle when he enters the comfortable environs of the airliner.

The traveler would experience a shocking jolt, however, if he were to find that certain provisions or preparations had been neglected. If the pilot had decided not to show up, if flight attendants were not cheerfully engaged in their tasks, if the airline personnel appeared to be in confusion, the passenger would give serious thought to the matter of traveling anywhere.

I'M READY, FLY ME

The efforts of a large number of people and extensive expenditures have gone into the planning for air travel. The takeoff, flight, and landing are merely the obvious areas for which planning must be made. No one would desire to fly if he were to suspect that the airline company had not made adequate preparations for the entire flight.

It is fair and reasonable to expect people to take no unnecessary chances with their lives. The pioneers of major endeavors, however, must possess a certain uncommon courage, else no significant accomplishment could ever take place.

The same apparently paradoxical situation exists in education: parents do not wish to subject their children to an untried innovation; none view their offspring as guinea pigs, and none should be expected to. Yet there has been enough background study, enough preparation, and certainly enough evidence of sound educational practice in the concept of continuous progress education to merit its trial in any community desiring an improved educational opportunity for their children. The firm counsel, however, is that the implementers prepare thoroughly before the program is inaugurated.

Actual implementation may be successful with the development of certain procedures and skills. To implement an individualized program, the teacher must first develop two skills: (1) he must master the art of writing objectives in behavioral terms, and (2) he must be able to identify major concepts and sub-concepts in his discipline, and, from this beginning, must develop the ability to make learning activity packages (see Chapter 7). These are the basic tools for the launching; other skills must be developed to maintain the ship on its voyage and to bring it to its destination. Within the well-constructed LAP (learning activities package) are the other tasks essential to the journey.

If continuous progress education is to be launched by an entire school, few sources could provide better guidance than that provided by the directors of the Model Schools Project. Under the direction of Dr. J. Lloyd Trump, his associate Dr. William Georgiades, and others, a number of high schools throughout the United States are engaged in developing curricula in which continuous progress education might be possible for every student. These schools are in various stages of curricular development, each endeavoring, as they are able, to implement individualized learning as it is set forth in the Model. The MSP Model, the general designation for this project, outlines the implementation tasks from every angle. In fact, the Model is set forth first as a program which takes into consideration three major principles. It is depicted in a triangle:

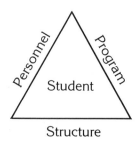

The student, obviously, is central to the program. The three factors surrounding the student encompass the complete task of this project. Concentrating on one of these factors, while excluding or neglecting either or both of the other factors, would predestine the project to failure. Each of these three sides of the triangle encompasses several elements essential to the success of the project.

A MODEL FLIGHT PATTERN

Let's look first at the **program.** At the heart of the program is a curriculum which includes: the structure (or framework) of each discipline outlining the essential knowledge needed by all; special interest or hobby areas for the student who is interested in more than the basic essentials; and information on careers as well as actual career opportunities for those who desire to pursue that direction.

The program sets forth three facets to the teaching-learning pattern: large group instruction for motivational purposes; small group reaction discussions for the purposes of student interaction and reaction to topics and issues; and independent study (some would label it "directed study") in which the student moves at his own rate through study guides (or learning activities packages) developed by the teacher. The LAPs provide a variety of learning strategies designed to accord with the interests and abilities of the learner.

Both administration and staff are concerned with the location of learning and teaching. The school plant is divided into various areas for study and work. In addition, study is made of the community and the home in an effort to determine the best places for optimal learning. It is readily conceded that the classroom itself may not be the best place for every learning experience.

At the heart of this curriculum (or program) is the point of view that learning is not to be restricted or relegated to a fixed period of time. Instead of time, performance (or achievement) becomes the major component of evaluation. This change of emphasis places a larger responsibility upon the learner—a position that is educationally sound. The student of English who "ain't learned nothin' all year" doesn't have anyone to blame but himself.

The **personnel,** basic to any curricular design, are especially significant in the MSP Model.

The administrative staff is so organized as to allow the principal to allot up to three-fourths of his time to instructional improvement. As the leader goes, so goes the school. Where his primary concern is picking up papers in the hall, the students will keep him occupied. If he has little concern for the curriculum, the teachers will develop their own and the total staff will likely be riding off in every direction; though none will be looking for the sunset, it will soon be a dark day for learning. The contention is that if the chief administrator is concerned primarily with student learning, the entire school will share the same concern.

A differentiated instructional staff is established in which teachers are occupied primarily with teaching-learning tasks. Other related tasks become the work of instructional assistants, clerical aides, and general aides. The costs for this differentiated staff are not greater than those for a conventional staff. The advantages are seen in the larger number of persons, each involved in the work for which he is prepared or which he can handle adequately. The professional educator is released to occupy his time fully with the professional tasks of instruction.

The Model includes also a plan for an efficient utilization of counseling personnel. At first this will bring dismay to the economy minded. Can schools afford such an array of counselors? The obvious answer is that a school should incorporate what it can. The design, however, makes academic sense.

Basic to the counseling pattern is the counseling role of the teacher-adviser. The teacher-adviser, an instructional staff member, is given approximately twenty-five to thirty counselees with whom he works throughout their secondary years (unless some changes must necessarily be made). The adviser assists each student in his class scheduling, evaluates his academic progress, and is generally on top of matters regarding the total experience of his student counselee. The teacher-adviser is the one who becomes acquainted with the total student. He communicates with the parents and is generally responsible for helping the student gain a sense of direction and an optimum amount of success in his school experience.

The professional counselor and the special consultants have their respective roles as well. They do not, however, occupy their time in the areas in which the teacher-adviser works. Advising in the areas of scholarship, academic matters, discipline, and personal problems is the major role of the counselor, but important qualities of any good counselor are his ability to recognize his own limitations and his readiness to make referrals when help is needed. The special consultant may be called in when the professional counselor senses the need to make referrals. The special consultant will likely not be a staff member; however, they should be available to the school and its students.

Structure is the third major ingredient of the MSP Model. Here the design takes a new look at the uses of time, space, and money; in addition, it frees the educator and learner from the conventional numbers in education—whether these numbers involve student-teacher ratios or the number of students involved in each learning opportunity provided by the school. The theme of the MSP Model as it relates to structure may be seen in the concepts of flexibility and learning options.

More specifically, time is no longer the pacemaker of the learning process; the student's pace is not interrupted to wait for his peers. His schedule for each discipline area (or subject) is varied according to his needs or interests. Along with his teacher-adviser, he varies the time allotments from week to week as the need is recognized.

A careful study of numbers and size is also made. The traditional thirty students per class is recognized for what it is—too large for small group discussion and too small (in some cases) for efficient large group presentations. Large groups, rightly controlled and brought together for the right purposes, can provide effective learning opportunities and be more efficient than the traditional class size. Other adjustments, small groups and independent study time, provide the bases for individualized, continuous progress education. Freed from the restrictions of five classes per week, thirty students per class, and from the continually lecturing teacher, the school becomes an opportunity center for individuals.

Furthermore, in the MSP Model the discussion of school space takes on a practical bent. It no longer presents the either-or argument over the open concept or the closed concept. It recognizes the need for a certain openness in the actual physical space and a certain open attitude toward the student; the latter concept involves confidence in the learner's desire to learn. On the other hand, it sees the need for a partly closed atmosphere as well; that is, it sees the student's need for some privacy, some place to go where he may occasionally be alone.

Thus, the MSP Model focuses on providing optimum learning opportunities for each learner. To do this, it insists on the importance of (1) the program of learning, (2) the personnel involved (and a proper utilization of the people of education), and (3) the structure necessary to implement individualized learning. The directors insist on the inclusion of all three factors in producing individualized, continuous progress education.

COMMONSENSE IMPLEMENTATION

Other proponents of individualized, continuous progress education have their unique approaches to the implementation task. Whatever approach may be employed, the educator should not forget two principles which emerge from this discussion.

One is that the developers of an individualized program of instruction will need to recognize the unique nature of the school and community in which they are working; from this realization they will adopt and adapt the concepts as these concepts fit the local setting.

The second principle suggests that innovators look at all three sides of the MSP triangle (if they choose to follow the MSP Model). For example, concentration on flexible scheduling and classroom space is not sufficient; this is where many earlier innovations fell short. Innovators must view both personnel and structural elements in inaugurating a program of learning which meets the individual needs of the learner.

Some may view us as naive realists or day-dreaming idealists. However, we must insist on doing only those things that can be done at the moment—on taking innovative steps one at a time, and on maintaining a sense of the direction toward which those steps lead us.

Common sense would remind us of another consideration as well—a fact of which the instructional staff should be aware. They should realize that, although much has been written about individualization of instruction, most of the hard work of preparing behavioral objectives and learning packages will need to be done by the local instructional staff. Many educators are waiting for "some-one, somewhere" to provide all this for them. It is true that much material has been developed; and in the well-worn phrase, we need not re-invent the wheel, there is an element of truth. However, no educator who is at a considerable distance from the local educational scene can know the basic needs, interests, and abilities of the students and the community as can the competent local educator on the scene. Most of the creative work of implementation will have to be done in the ball park in which the game is to be played.

How does the
teacher set the
climate for creative
learning...?

CLEARING THE AIR 15
AND SETTING
THE CLIMATE

Implementation of individualized learning involves establishing an academic climate conducive to clear, creative thinking.

THE WRONG CLIMATE

Most teachers, perhaps all teachers, find it difficult to start students on their way to creative thinking. Unnoticed by the majority of these teachers is the fact that their own basic approaches tend to discourage the activity they wish to inspire. Among those practices that fail to enhance creativity are:

1. Administering tests and quizzes based on lectures and textbook assignments.
2. Assigning marks (or letter grades) based on test results.
3. Assuming an authoritative role in the classroom, where truth is measured by agreement with the teacher's point of view.
4. Giving praise and other immediate rewards for correct answers.
5. Rebuking those with wrong answers or those who apparently failed to fulfill the assignment.
6. Displaying uneasiness when material is not "covered" in the expected amount of time.

7. Viewing with suspicion the student who is slow to agree with the teacher's point of view.
8. Placing undue emphasis on knowledge at the cognitive level of learning opportunities.
9. Insisting on an exact procedure for problem solving.
10. Displaying impatience with discussions which do not seem to relate directly to the subject.
11. Lacking curiosity and failing to study, and thereby allowing the development of a barren learning environment.
12. Acting on the desire to help the student by presenting answers for the student too readily. (This is the "pity for the chicken in the shell" syndrome.)
13. Assuming that opportunities for creative experiences are to be reserved for the gifted students—that average and slow students should complete their assignments first.
14. Assuming accountability for the learning experiences of the student, and failing to place the appropriate amount of responsibility for learning upon the student.

It should not be concluded that all of the practices listed above are altogether bad. Under certain conditions some of the practices cited may be acceptable educational procedures. (This may be true of numbers 1 through 4, 10, and 12.) It is when the teacher permits these practices or attitudes to set the predominate tone of the classroom that he defeats his own efforts to promote a climate for creativity.

SETTING THE RIGHT CLIMATE

How, then, does the teacher set the climate for creative learning? What steps can be consciously and conscientiously taken?

First, the teacher must become a thorough student, developing a fascination for the subject area or discipline in which he teaches. Wherever possible, he should avoid teaching in an area in which he has little interest.

He should take a new view of his students. He should develop an honest, humane attitude toward each—not alone toward the likable, positive, friendly student. He needs to place a high value on each student; and he should recognize that the mind of even the slow learner is a marvelous instrument. Even the slow learner has the power to think (not merely reflect) and to do. When the teacher can honestly take this view of the student, a large barrier between student and teacher is removed and a major step toward creative learning takes place.

Another step may be taken by removing the silence-immobility barrier. Some teachers hold the antiquated concept that children in school should be both silent and still. We concede that noise and movement are not necessarily equated with a good learning climate, but natural movement and even excited conversation may be vital to the active participant in the learning experience. Perhaps the sole criterion regulating this factor should be courtesy—a courtesy that governs the climate so that each student may enjoy an optimum learning experience.

Even though the objectives and the directions of the learning experiences may be very clearly outlined (for both the student and the teacher), the teacher should allow and even encourage the students to take different routes. The learning experience has often been equated with a journey; not all take the same route to get from one place to another; nor do all use the same mode of travel. The teacher should recognize and honor the individual differences of his students, while encouraging each student to discover more and more effective means for proceeding on the academic journey.

The teacher should recognize and help the student recognize that the classroom is merely the rallying place in which learning journeys begin. In itself, the classroom is a barren place enlivened only by the active minds of the learners—teachers and students. To establish effective, continuous learning the teacher must open up the world environment to the student—the immediate community and the larger community—the environment that includes peoples of all ages, society, institutions, industries, recreational facilities and nature. By contrast, the classroom with its chalkboard, desks, bulletin boards, and textbooks is an environmentally deprived area.

The teacher should develop (not fear) the concepts of fun and serendipity in the learning experience. The old stereotype of the teacher and students suffering embarrassment when the principal walks in during a time of laughter or when students are moving to various parts of the room, should not continue as a normal reaction. A happy, accidental discovery should not be the experience solely of the scientist. Developing this climate helps remove an unfortunate clinical correctness—that is, the concept that the student has to come up with the right answer or suffer the embarrassment of being wrong. The scientist has the right to be wrong often. If the privilege were given to the student, he would interact verbally with others far more readily, and learning would be enhanced. The teacher should not allow any inner insecurity to funnel a student's thought into a narrow, unhappy, constricted area. Opportunities for ideas to pop up should be welcomed.

If creativity is ever to develop, the student should be introduced to the experience of meditation and reflection. This is not the idle daydream; nor is it a waste of precious time. Here, in the experience of reflection, man is at his greatest. This experience is gained through worship and through appreciation of nature; the Scriptures, the great books, the people whom we love, the problems that confront us, all provide opportunities for meditation and reflection. Such is the nature of meditation and creation that its activity and processes cannot be outlined or analyzed successfully. The experience, however, is more readily created in students whose teachers do all in their power to develop the appropriate climate.

The creative mind frightens many of us; yet if we have helped establish the proper climate, if we have introduced the learner to great values (social, intellectual, and spiritual), then we need not fear the creation of a monster. The reflective student will create "a thing of beauty" which is (in the eyes of the wise man) "a joy forever."

He must not take himself so seriously
that he begins to assume the role of a prophet
facing a den of lions daily.

A PROPHET WITHOUT PROFIT

16

If you feel brave enough to be an innovator, and we hope you are, you must be as willing to bear the consequences of innovative attempts as you are to reap the rewards or receive the plaudits when innovative efforts prove fruitful.

The major consideration in tipping the scale toward innovative practices or away from them should be the welfare of the young learner. If something must be done to improve his learning opportunities, then you must do it. If the slow learner's present and future hope for success is contingent upon your stepping forth with a valid concept, then you must step forth. To refuse to take such a step for fear of some scurrilous label that might be placed on you may be cowardly and, in a graver sense, immoral. This is not to say that anyone not engaged in innovative practices is an academic and moral weakling. It is saying, however, that whenever you value personal reputation above the needs of young learners, you are facing a moral crisis.

Today the world of education needs educators who are willing to take reasonable chances for the purpose of bringing improved learning opportunities to our children and youth. In most cases, the consequences of minor innovative failures are not unbearable. Certain labels may be attached to your name, or the public (including educators) might form certain mental images of you. It is when these labels or mental images are negative or inaccurate that we get up tight. Perhaps fear of failure is not so great as our fear of being the recipients of improper labels or of being mentally caricatured as educational buffoons.

MAINTAINING A SENSE OF HUMOR

The truth of the matter is that whether we sit still or move ahead, we are the recipients of undesirable labels and images. So the innovator needs to develop a wholesome sense of humor in which he can readily laugh at himself. He must not take himself so seriously that he begins to assume the role of a prophet who feels that he is daily facing a den of lions. There are few more unfortunate spectacles than an inflexible, self-pitying innovator who intones with solemn incantations precisely what must be done to change the existing evils of education.

To pontificate against existing practices may be one way of bringing about change, but it is certainly not the best way. It is better to bring in a new idea on a positive note, presenting it as a fascinating idea with limitless possibilities. We believe this to be true of continuous progress education.

We have little affinity with those critics of education who paint a cloud of gloom over existing educational practices, but who have very few alternatives to offer. They and we need to offer that "new affection" toward which educators and learners might be attracted.

We need to take reasonable chances, for in most cases, their potential consequences are not generally cataclysmic. In addition, we need to be ready to accept failures along the way. Failures are often no worse than stepping stones to ultimate success. The failure which comes from trying is not so great as the failure to try; the first is the experience of being wounded in action, while the latter is the experience of dying from inaction. Sometimes innovators may be guilty of playing the role of educational cheerleaders; even here, however, the role is healthy, for it depicts vigorous mental action.

WHO NEEDS AN UNPROFITABLE PROPHET?

It is the prophet of doom who cannot profit; it is the one who discourages and who holds back who makes it difficult to move forward. The educator who is against change is, in a sense, against education—for education, by definition, involves change.

If your failing efforts do no real damage to a learner, but only to your ego, you might either cry or laugh. The latter option is more rewarding, for it not only reflects a healthier outlook, but it tends not to close the doors to new ideas. And should someone label you "a walking behavioral objective" or "a dreamer in the cognitive domain," you can at least be assured that you have a sense of direction and that you possess certain values. Perhaps the following lines depict the seriousness with which you might view your failures:

AN ODE TO INNOVATION

Please, fellow educator, would you please refrain
    From referring again to that cognitive domain?
And, furthermore, I just really have to confess
    I've had enough of accountability and the P.P.B.S.

I've heard so very much of this individualized instruction
    The lack of which, I've contributed to the kid's destruction.
Just how can an old teacher his self image contain
    For when he attempts to discipline, he's really inhumane?

I'm told that continuous progress is the way to go
    And how in 'n out of my class the kids'll ever flow.
And, as for teaching—well, don't be so dumb,
    It's not you that matters; it's the learning outcome.

Furthermore, you don't put grades on a report card
    For on the kid's constitution, it's just too hard.
And, never, no never, do you paddle or slap
    For you'll destroy his ego, and widen the gap.

Parents get upset, and their hearts go to bleeding
    Whenever they hear of their kid's poor, poor reading.
But the facts are, if you really care to look,
    It's been years since the parents ever read a good book.

As for teaching methodology, the contract's "in,"
    The learning activity package is its next of kin.
But cross-age teaching is the real goat getter,
    Cause it says that as a teacher, a kid's much better.

The modern cafeteria provides education with its model
    And it can cause any non-drinker to grab for the bottle.
Alternatives are to range from traditional to school that's open
    For ways to implement all this, we are still blindly gropin'.

Now, the learner does the selecting, it's just got to be,
    For far wiser than the educator is the educatee.
And, I understand, learning's a journey from here to there,
    So to start without objectives, you just don't dare.

The administrator does his part, and don't you dare laugh,
    He juggles teachers 'n aides; calls it utilization of staff.
If there's a stupid kid in class, you've nothing to fear
    For he's studying school administration as his future career.

So come large group, small group, and flexible time module,
    For this is what it's about in the up-to-date school.
Be open to change, to any modality—even to teaming
    In the serenity of your soul, enjoy the kids' screaming.

As innovative, enthusiastic educators, let us have malice only toward inertia; let us enjoy the results of serendipity, and welcome the consequences of innovation.

PART FOUR

APOLOGIA

They speak freely of the ideas
that were tried but did not succeed.

WAYWARD SHOTS 17
THAT MISS
THE MOOSE

When anyone sets forth a proposal to which he has given much attention and study, he becomes somewhat defensive as critics begin to attack the proposal. Actually, the one who sets forth the proposal should welcome the critics' attacks. These attacks provide the refining fire that helps the innovator forge a proposal that will endure the tests of reality. If the proposal cannot endure, it deserves the death of the unqualified. Most innovators should admit that their ideas are colored with personal prejudice; the innovator does not always have the objectivity that he needs. For these reasons and others he should welcome the voice of the critics.

We who propose continuous progress education as a valid approach to dynamic learning have had to field a number of questions and criticisms. Without being defensive we will attempt to answer some of the questions of the critics.

THE SHOTS

Most concerned, dedicated teachers come up with a question much like this: "In an effort to individualize, how can you possibly get to every student as often as you should?"

Our answer is that you likely cannot get to each student as often as you feel you should. But the very fact that you realize his individual needs is an improvement over the traditional or conventional program. Furthermore, the student may not need individual attention as often as you might think. It is very possible, as has been suggested previously, that you can deal with his individual needs in small groups. The significant points are that you are recognizing his individual needs and attempting to prescribe those activities that will help him. You must keep in mind also that skills in this area will grow. Materials will be acquired and approaches will be developed that will give you increasing skills in the individualization of instruction. The teacher can be certain that his attempts to individualize instruction are attempts that face him in the right direction as a teacher.

Another valid question is one concerned with costs. "Isn't continuous progress education or individualized instruction very costly?"

No doubt any changeover from one program to another will involve initial costs that are not generally a part of the conventional program. However, any program of education which is well thought through may provide areas in which the educator might economize. Administrators, for example, may economize through the proper utilization of staff. There are many activities in the learning setting which do not require the supervision of professional educators. Adults of various qualifications may be hired to do those tasks. This cost should be considerably lower than that of a professional educator. Some look at the cost of materials involved. Here again, materials need not be professionally developed materials. Also, the sharing of materials can go on among teachers and between districts. Teacher-developed materials may be much more effective than commercially produced materials. Again, we need to recognize this as a growing experience in which materials are developed, accumulated, refined and used with increasing effectiveness.

Another concern is the one that comes to us in a question of this nature: "But what should happen if we run out? Suppose the student goes through the learning experiences we have developed and suppose we cannot keep up with his needs."

It would be inane for any lady to complain that her money buys too much at the grocery store. No housewife would complain if she were to find money left over to purchase items she hadn't thought she could afford. In spite of all the jokes the male chauvinist might concoct, it would be difficult to come up with one containing such a punch line.

Yet there are those who have serious reservations about the workability of continuous progress education who have come up with questions depicting an equally ridiculous concern. Perhaps the concern is momentary; certainly it has not been thought through carefully. The concern is often framed in questions such as: "Suppose the kids get through all the learning materials prepared for them?" "Won't some kids rush through the learning materials to see how rapidly they can finish?" "Won't the kids who finish early cause problems for the teacher and the other kids?"

Imbedded in each of these questions is the common thought that we need to hold kids back to a pace that will stretch the course out over a full year. This suggests that the time requirement we have placed upon learning is sacred. It implies that we know that each student should spend a full twelve or thirteen years in school (K through 12). This concern actually encourages resistance to learning. It tells the student to cool it: "Young learner, you've got nine months to learn decimals, so take it easy; you don't get algebra until the ninth grade."

One of the questions above may have a degree of merit; the one concerned with learners rushing through the materials. We too would oppose slip-shod, careless learning experiences. We agree that mastery at each step should be thorough and lasting. But does it terrify us that a student might go much farther in his twelve year learning journey than may have been required? If the student, along with his tax-paying parents, should desire more learning per tax dollar, should we view that as a problem to eradicate? If a curricular approach, namely continuous progress education, should bring about this change in the student's attitude toward learning, is it to be resisted? The transfer of student values away from ego-boosting grades (or ego-destroying grades) to a concern for learning should be one of the major objectives of education; it is a major objective of continuous progress education.

A LOOK AT THE MOOSE

Somewhere in the distant past most of us have studied the great paintings of famous artists. Among the paintings many of us have encountered is Sir Edwin Landseer's **Monarch of the Glen,** a work depicting a magnificent moose in his mountainous, wooded environment. Since art brings a variety of experiences to different viewers, hopefuly there are those who have an aesthetic experience of this painting. But we can imagine some viewers who, upon looking at the moose, are reminded of their insurance needs, and others who dream of getting such a magnificent animal in the sights of a powerful rifle—to them the animal is a trophy to be shot down.

It is the second group that represents a large segment of professional educators and the reading public. To this group, innovations are merely moose to be shot down. They enjoy having moose heads on the walls of their dens (often the most appropriately named room in their homes). They speak freely of ideas that were tried but did not succeed. They can relate the place and the year in which the innovation was launched; and with an educated, experienced finality they can administer the coup-de-grace to any new idea by declaring that it was tried in the past and just didn't work. Seldom do such observers admit that they were among those who took shots at the moose.

As educators view the composite picture of continuous progress education, they very likely see several vulnerable spots.

At the heart of the matter, for example, is the cost factor; seemingly here is where continuous progress education can be shot down in a hurry. Or is this really the case? We would remind you to recall three basic considerations:

First, the actual dollars and cents cost need not be permanently greater than a conventional program. We have attempted to illustrate this through the proper utilization of the teaching staff. The Model Schools Project makes this clear (see Trump and Georgiades, "Doing Better With What You Have—NASSP Model Schools Project"). A reduction of professional teachers accompanied by an increase of nonprofessional or paraprofessional adult help can provide an individualized program with little or no increase in salary costs. Furthermore, we need not insist on costly new buildings, for much can be done within the old physical framework.

A second consideration, when tabulating the costs of education, is the measurement of learning outcomes. If the learning outcomes are greater over the span of years, cannot that be an indication of economy? There is evidence that this consideration is more than a mere conditional "if." (See Ovard, "The Practitioner's Guide to Research.")

A third consideration about cost takes into account the change in values brought about through continuous progress education. Here the value is placed on learning rather than grades; the value is placed on individuals rather than impersonal groups; the emphasis, from the teacher's point of view, is on the progress of every learner; further emphases are on the learner's responsibilities for his own learning, on the learner's creativity and problem solving abilities, and on his understanding of the learning process (that he might be able to research a problem or an unfamiliar task). In the long run, it is not a costly maneuver to educate people who can go on learning when the teacher is not there. To educate people who have mastered certain tools of learning is not as costly as to see merely that a learner gets a B.A. with a B average. (Come to think of it, that's about all this latter individual will amount to; he will "be average.")

RECLEANING THE GUN

If there is any Achilles heel in continuous progress education, the moose hunters would say, it is in the behavioral objective. Here is where they would say the whole idea breaks down. "After all, you cannot write objectives for all learning experiences; there are certain intangibles, certain feelings, personal values, and subliminal areas of the learner's experience that the teacher cannot invade, let alone measure."

We have previously dealt rather extensively with objectives and will not repeat ourselves here. However, before concluding that the behavioral objective is the Achilles heel of continuous progress education, we should reevaluate its vulnerability. First, as we examine Bloom's taxonomy we find six major areas or levels of the intellect (the cognitive domain). We find it possible to write behavioral objectives at every level of the intellect. Next, we look at Krathwohl's taxonomy in the affective domain—the domain of values and attitudes. Again, we find that we can write objectives dealing with values. Admittedly, this task is not as easy as the first. But if our objectives are not measurable in the sense that we can place them in percentage categories, they may at least be observable. In these instances the evaluations are made from observations. In addition to this, where we get into intensely personal areas of response the learner can be given opportunity to measure his learning experiences. He may be given opportunities for expression (through writing, speaking, drawing, and so on) that will reveal the impact of the learning experience on his life.

This leads us to a conclusion that may appear foolhardy to some: rather than being the Achilles heel of continuous progress education, the behavioral objective is actually a far better tool for clarifying the learning experiences to be gained than has been realized. When educators state that there is a lot of learning with which the behavioral objective cannot deal, they have not yet considered all the possible dimensions and applications of behavioral objectives.

A conscientious educator, whether classroom teacher or harried administrator, may make the plaintive plea, "After all, isn't it expecting pretty much of an educator to adopt a personalized, individualized, continuous progress program of education?"

In response, we must admit that few worthwhile programs are easy. We must also be as humane with educators as we are with learners. Our answer, we trust, is couched in common sense: "We implement as we are able; we employ when we are ready." The key words are "progress" and "growth"; each of these takes time.

Other shots have been (and could be) taken at continuous progress education, but we've spent enough time dodging the bullets. It will be much more profitable to get on with the task.

Basically, the problem of grading is merely a surface issue.

MORE ON EVALUATION OR MORON GRADING? 18

In education a clear distinction needs to be made between grades or marks and evaluation. Debates over grades have gone on for some time. Should we get rid of grades? Should we modify or change the grading system? Several solutions have been proposed and implemented, yet real satisfaction has not been reached. For example, in many areas proponents of the pass-fail system have gained headway. Yet, when analyzed, this system does not solve the grading problem. It comes up short for at least three reasons: (1) It retains the fail problem. (2) It cuts down on the motivation factor in grading; it doesn't encourage excellence in learning. (3) It retains essentially the same grading system that is under attack; the sole difference is that there are fewer degrees on the learning thermometer.

Much more could be said of the grading problem, but the problem of grading is merely a surface issue. The fact that we have the problem of grades is an indication that the teaching-learning program has a basically wrong thrust. If it were our purpose to teach facts, to teach at the knowledge level of the cognitive domain, then the old grading system we have had may be the best system of evaluation (or at least as good as any other system for measuring the learning of facts).

The point we wish to stress in this book, however, is that while there are numerous points of view regarding grading, the real issue arises from the fact that basic to all effective learning experiences is evaluation.

EVALUATION DISTINGUISHED FROM GRADES

Grades may be viewed by some as a nuisance factor, by others as an extrinsic motivator, by others as the means of receiving praise and acclaim. But evaluation is an integral part of the planning for learning, the learning experience itself, the necessary adjustments and corrections in learning, and the outcomes of the teaching-learning experience.

We can see quite readily how evaluation is woven as a thread throughout the learning experience. Evaluation is basic to:

1. Diagnosis. This involves a determination of the learner's readiness to engage in the particular learning experience.
2. Placement on the continuum or sequence of the learning ladder.
3. A validation of learning objectives to determine their relationship to the philosophy of the educational system and to student needs.
4. Feedback. Frequent if not continuous feedback is needed to determine the degree and nature of the learner's progress.
5. Planning further learning experiences.
6. Sound accountability. Realistic evaluation examines the performance of the student, the efficiency of the means used in reaching this performance level, and even the cost factors in the learning experience.
7. The total operation of the school system. Evaluation probes not only student needs and progress, but teacher methods, relationships, and effectiveness. Furthermore, it examines the school curriculum, the administration, and the soundness of the entire school program.
8. Reliable permanent records. As the student passes from one level to another, accurate records of the growth, needs, and progress of each student must be kept. These records enable educators to evaluate past progress, to correct incorrect procedures, and to plot future learning.
9. Counseling and guidance. The more effective and accurate the evaluating system, the more effective and relevant will be the counsel. It becomes an effective tool in guiding the student and in keeping the parent informed of problems and progress.

FACING REALITY IN EVALUATION

One of the startling realities of education today is the paucity of significant systems for evaluating the effectiveness of educational procedures. In introducing new programs, we have long relied on the

Hawthorne effect as the evidence of how a program is working—if everyone is elated, if the teachers are happy and the kids seem to like it, we label the practice a success. When the enthusiasm dies down, we skip back into the old routines; and when another innovator comes storming in, we cool his ardor with, "Well, we've tried it once."

This brings us to the realities we must face in establishing a continuous progress program of education. Three facts of evaluation are certain in such an endeavor. One is that a sound, careful, accurate system of evaluation must be established to measure student needs, progress, and growth. Another is that teachers and administrators must be willing to adopt a positive attitude towards evaluation of their work and its effectiveness. Rightly established, evaluation is for the purpose of aiding the teacher in his professional growth. An evaluative structure that can help the teacher become more effective and competent should be welcomed. The administrator must assume the same attitude.

Third, the educational system should be subjected to a means for determining sound statistical evidences of its effectiveness or ineffectiveness. These evidences should not probe only cognitive growth. A basic question should be, "Is the system employed meeting not only the academic needs, but also the social, physical, and moral needs of the student?"

So if we were to return to that simple question, "Should we get rid of grades?" our answer could be "Yes, "No," "Maybe," or "I'm not certain." But if we were to ask, "Should we get rid of evaluation?" the answer must be, "Never!" Evaluation is that means by which we get to know our students and ourselves. It is basic to our students' growth and to our own.

Our flexible schedules have
scarcely been more effective than to show off
our vaunted academic strength.

BEWARE OF INFLEXIBLE FLEXIBILITY

19

There are few practices more inflexible than a number of the so-called "flexible" schedules of recent decades. For a time, the popular thing to do in our schools (to reveal our innovative spirit) was to "flex our schedules." We have been much like the boy who flexes his muscles to show off his strength. The boy may not be willing to put his muscles to useful work, but he is very ready to brag of his strength.

FLEXING OUR MUSCLES
Our flexible schedules have scarcely been more effective than to show off our vaunted academic strength. Soon challenges began to knock the chips off our shoulders and to demand proof of our strength (enter the ogre—accountability!).

Flexibility has sounded too "in"—it's been just the thing to do in order to be on the cutting edge in promoting meaningful educational experiences. But we needed to ask ourselves a few questions: "Just what are we trying to do in education? In what way can flexible scheduling improve the learning experience? Why have we adopted a flexible schedule?"

No doubt, some good has come from these flexible schedules. The monotony has been broken up. Teachers have had opportunity for more extensive preparation. Mini-courses and special curriculum offerings have been introduced. But all of these, though helpful, do not quite get to the heart of the matter.

What is the basic purpose of flexibility? If we move in the direction of flexible scheduling for the purpose of meeting the individual needs of all learners that they might continually progress in the most efficient manner, we have identified a valid purpose. And yet, to accomplish our purpose, we suspect that flexibility must involve more than a flexibility in scheduling.

THE SCOPE OF FLEXIBILITY

If ever a curriculum design is to pave the way for continuous progress education, it must have a flexibility that reaches far beyond the schedule alone. Among the areas in which flexibility is essential to continuous progress education are the following:

1. First, of course, is the flexible schedule. This should not be the "pseudo-flexible" schedule that merely locks the student into a pattern considerably different from the traditional six periods a day for five days a week. The schedule should provide for the varied needs of the student to the extent that it allows him to spend the **time** he needs and to spend it **where** he needs to be, for the learning experience.

2. There must be great flexibility in the utilization of the professional teaching staff. If the teacher is bound to a rigid program—a certain number of assigned study halls, numerous clerical duties, and other tasks only dimly related to teaching—flexibility will be lacking. The staff needs to be supplemented by other personnel—teaching aides, assistants, and other adult personnel. In some cases older students might be utilized. (See the **Model School Project** in Trump and Georgiades, "NASSP Model Schools Action Program," for suggestions on utilization of staff.)

3. Teachers must employ flexible teaching procedures that allow for individualized learning experiences. Teachers cannot remain front and center five days per week and ever hope to develop a continuous progress program for individual students.

4. Flexibility in teacher placement is essential. If the employing organization or the teacher should insist on rigid placement, continuous progress education would neither continue nor progress. By this we mean that a teacher cannot limit his range to teaching only at the sixth grade level or only at the senior level in the high school. A teacher should be professionally prepared to relate to students on a range of levels, possibly Levels 8 through 15 in a particular subject area, Levels 7 through 12 in another discipline, and so on. (This would vary according to the

structure of the disciplines.) A teacher insisting on teaching in the sixth grade alone would immediately throw a banana peel in the path of continuous progress education. (We couldn't afford such monkeying around!) The span of learners under the charge of a particular teacher might range over several levels in the continuous progress continuum. In essence, teachers are needed who are generalists in that they deal with a rather broad spectrum of learners; they are to be specialists, however, in setting up learning experiences for students, in preparing materials, in evaluating student placement and progress, and in diagnosing student needs and interests.

5. Administrators must be prepared to harmonize the needs for flexibility in continuous progress education. This may involve: (a) scheduling the uses of the school plant itself—the classrooms, laboratories, and other facilities; (b) changing the design or physical features of the classrooms; (c) working out the curriculum schedules more often than at the beginning of each semester; and (d) maintaining the attendance records—a complicated task under this design, for schools must be accountable for knowing where students are while allowing them enough freedom of movement to pursue their learning experiences.

6. Flexibility as it relates to time must be understood. In the past we have allowed a magic formula to prevail: appropriate courses over a nine-month period produce so many semester periods of credit (or Carnegie Units); a course completed at the adequate grade level means the task is completed; if a student has "had" certain courses, he is permitted to enter certain others. In such a system, the matter of competence, performance, or mastery is of little consequence.

   Yet there is no magic formula to insure that students can master Chemistry, English I, Typing I, Homemaking, or whatever in nine months. Why should a person be stigmatized for taking five years to master what ordinarily is considered to be the work in grades 9 through 12? Alternatively, why should a person be prevented from mastering that work in a shorter time? Is the four-year span an educational sacred cow? Flexibility about time allows us to place our stress on learning rather than on course completion.

7. Basic, but seldom considered, is the need for flexibility on the part of the student. He will need to assume more responsibility for learning, and he will need to discover those approaches to the learning task that are the most effective

under given situations. But most important (and hopefully not too much to ask), the student will need a willingness to begin his learning endeavors at the level at which he is best able to function. For example, let us suppose that at the end of a given school year a student has passed (or mastered) Level 15 in a given discipline. When he comes back in the autumn, however, he may recognize that he has not retained the mastery that would enable him to begin Level 16. The educational system should have helped him evaluate so that he would personally request returning to Level 15 until mastery could be assured. If he were to insist on going on to Level 16 without adequate preparation, it would be an indication that the concepts and values in continuous progress education had not been thoroughly established.

8. Flexibility must exist in the guidance of learners. Teachers, students, and parents must not only acknowledge individual differences but must plan the learning experiences to meet the needs of the different individuals. The demand that each individual be treated exactly as another individual is treated is a marvel of inconsistency. (If doctors were to try that in dealing with patients, the doctors would have far greater headaches than their patients!)

THE STRENGTH OF FLEXIBILITY

There are those who think of flexibility as a sign of weakness in an individual. Flexibility, or adaptability, is not to be equated with the experience of the batter in baseball who gets a "jelly leg" when the opposing pitcher throws a fast ball at his head. The batter is just plain scared.

By contrast, flexibility is a necessary element in a strong individual or in a well-planned program. The individual who becomes increasingly rigid in thought and practice eventually betrays a weakness (or insecurity) of character. It is right to stand rigidly for the right, but it is wrong to stand rigidly for the wrong when evidence against the stand may be overwhelming. The reed may bend with the wind and be viewed as weak, but it is far more capable of becoming the channel for life-giving air than is the inflexible, rigid stump of a tree.

Education involves change. If we can't change, our education will not only not **continue** to progress: it cannot even begin!

We bottle up our kids in a high-school program and age them for 4 years. Small wonder many blow their corks.

MINI-RESULTS AT MAXI-COSTS

20

We should never be brutal in our evaluation of one another, but there are times when we need to take an objective look at ourselves and at what we are accomplishing.

Too often we evaluate our accomplishments with instruments too shallow or dull to provide accurate measurements—it's much like tilling the soil with a teaspoon. One of these teaspoons is the enthusiastic proclamation, "The students like it, and the teachers are happy with it." This permits us to settle into the rut of self satisfaction; but it prevents us from getting to the root of evaluation.

Can you and I be brave enough to take a real look at what we are doing in education? A student generally takes five "solid" subjects each year. The cost of his education is approximately $1,000 per year (this varies extensively, but the figure cited is a "ball park" figure). Each subject area, then, comes at a price of about $200. What has the student received, done, or learned for $200? In our course he has read one book. Would you pay $200 for the privilege of reading a book? When we realize that some students haven't even cracked the book, we have reason for more dismay! To soften the blow to our wounded sense of accountability, we remind ourselves that there has been much more to the course than the mere reading of the book. We've kept the student in the course for 180 days; we've required a couple of term papers (that is, if we are tough teachers); the student has been quizzed and tested; and he has had interaction experiences with students and teacher. But what has the student learned? We are not sure. As a matter of fact, we're not sure of what we wanted him to learn! The 180 days, the term papers, quizzes, tests, and discussions have not really assured us of anything.

However, one reality can be salvaged in this educational pattern; we can be quite sure that the good student will have mastered one formula—a formula he can apply to most course offerings: $GPA = ACT^2$ (grade point average equals the ability to con the teacher times the ability to cool the test). The tragedy is in the willingness of parents and students to pay an inordinate amount of money for a GPA that may not be the least bit transferable to the student's life goals and experiences.

Let's examine this course offering further. Are we justified in dragging out a course over a period of 180 days? Can we defend sentencing all students to the same term? (The nine-month period is sacred in very few areas of human development.) From this experience does the student gain a sense of individual responsibility? Does he gain an understanding of the value of time when time is so indiscriminately allocated as a requisite to learning?

As we probe further we strike another hard reality: the almost universal willingness to accept credits earned as a measure of academic progress—a poor substitute for skills attained or concepts mastered. Expressions such as "he has taken the course" or "she got her Master's degree" reveal where we have placed our values. Seldom have we designated learning as the measure of academic progress.

The intrusion of the word "accountability" into the educational scene, however, brings with it the demand that we look at learning as the major goal of education. Isn't it strange that this emphasis on learning outcomes should come as a comparatively new thought to many of us? Isn't it odd that we have objected to learning objectives in education? When we say that instructional objectives constitute another fad that will pass away, do we know what we are saying? Aren't we saying that we'll soon get back to the condition in which we have no sense of direction, we don't know where we're going, and we don't know how much it costs to get there? Aren't we buying mini-results at maxi-costs?

We bottle up our kids in a high school program and age them for four years. Small wonder many of them blow their corks! They, too, see only mini-results at maxi-costs.

It's time we learned educators examine our accomplishments realistically—and it's time to reverse the practice of getting mini-results at maxi-costs. We need the moxie to get the maxi out of the mini (our apologies to the 3M Corporation).

PART
FIVE

HOW
TO

HOW TO INVOLVE THE COMMUNITY, THE STUDENTS, AND THE STAFF

HOW TO INVOLVE THE COMMUNITY

INVOLVER

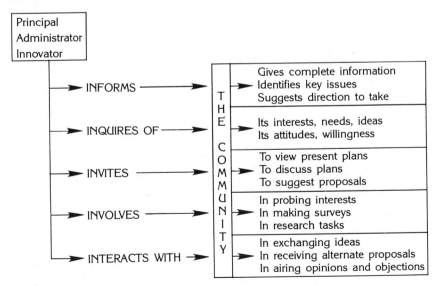

HOW TO INVOLVE THE STUDENTS

STEP ONE	Acknowledge that the educational program has need of improvement.
STEP TWO	Identify the purpose of the educational program under consideration.
STEP THREE	Introduce students to the new formula designed for individual needs.
STEP FOUR	Permit students to react, criticize, suggest ideas, and assist in planning.
STEP FIVE	Treat students as part of the community (Inform, Inquire, Invite, Involve, Interact).

HOW TO MOTIVATE THE STAFF

The administrator should:

1. Involve the staff in identifying reasons why change is needed.
2. Help teachers understand reasons for negative attitudes toward change.
3. Promote the concept that adopting new methods is not a condemnation of old methods.
4. Provide thorough orientation to concepts of continuous progress.
5. Allow reasonable time for attitude changes and concept acceptance to occur.
6. Involve the staff in planning changes.
7. Promote staff visitation to successfully operated continuous progress programs.
8. Seek staff agreement on essential tasks.
9. Assist teachers in mastering the three organizational skills required: (a) Developing sequential levels for each subject area, (b) Writing behavioral objectives, and (c) Developing Learning Activity Packages.

HOW TO STRUCTURE THE CURRICULUM AND DEVELOP AN INDIVIDUALIZED LEARNING DESIGN

HOW TO STRUCTURE THE CURRICULUM

We Look at Structure
1. Look at each discipline and determine how to organize it from K through 12.
2. Structure each discipline in terms of sequence, scope, and level.

We Look at the Level
1. Establish the level in terms of a major learning concept.
2. Preassess student competence in order to determine readiness for the level.
3. Write objectives to give direction to the learning.
4. Develop appropriate learning opportunities for each learner.
5. Set up self-testing opportunities for students.
6. Use teacher-made tests of student performance and readiness for the next level.

HOW TO DEVELOP AN INDIVIDUALIZED LEARNING DESIGN
(Two Views)

APPROACH A

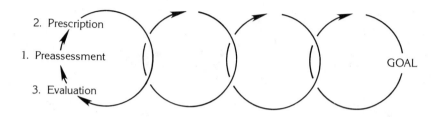

2. Prescription

1. Preassessment

3. Evaluation

GOAL

1. Preassessment: Determine student needs.
2. Prescription: Give appropriate assignments.
3. Evaluation: Measure student progress toward the goal.

APPROACH B
1. Assessment: Diagnose status of learner.
2. Prescription: Give learning assignments.
3. Instruction: Set up learning opportunities appropriate for each learner.
4. Evaluation: Evaluate student progress.

HOW TO DEVELOP PERFORMANCE OBJECTIVES

THE PERFORMANCE OBJECTIVE

The performance objective (or behavioral objective) is the basic tool the teacher should master in the development of a learning package.

1. It clarifies the learning task for the student.
2. It gives direction to the instructional task of the teacher.
3. It forms the basis for evaluating student progress.
   a. It is the basis for the pretest.
   b. It is the basis for the post-test.
   c. It is a basis for measuring teacher effectiveness.
4. For help in writing performance objectives see:
   a. The enclosed bibliography.
   b. The following outline on the writing of performance objectives.

WRITING PERFORMANCE OBJECTIVES

A number of teachers in recent years have been frightened by an ogre called the behavioral objective. Much of the blame for the psychological block that many teachers have experienced should be laid upon those professional educators who have made the writing of objectives appear to be such a difficult, technical task.

1. To begin writing performance objectives, a teacher may start by asking a few simple questions, such as: What is it that I hope to

teach the students in this course or unit? What do I expect each student to be able to do? What skills should he have? What principles should he understand?

2. Next, the teacher should write a simple statement describing what the student will do as a result of his learning experience.

3. The statement, or objective, should be clear to the student.

4. The results of the learning experience required in the objective should be measurable and/or observable.

5. Examples:

   a. "The student will recite the Bill of Rights from memory." This is an acceptable performance objective. One may not like the objective, it may not be the learning outcome one desires, but it does fulfill two basic principles found in a good objective: it indicates that the student, or learner, will accomplish something, and the requirement is clearly measurable or observable.

   b. "The student will write the names of the chemical elements known as halogens." The objective is simple, yet it contains the two elements cited above.

6. Each objective should move the student toward the goal of the unit. An objective that has nothing to do with the goal of the unit should be discarded.

7. After gaining confidence in writing the basic performance objective, the instructor may begin to expand on the objective by indicating the **conditions** under which the learner will perform and the **standards** (criteria) he is expected to reach. Example: In a **ten-minute test** (condition) the student will type at the rate of **30 words per minute** (standard).

8. As the teacher studies further he may, through using such works as Bloom's and Krathwohl's taxonomies, write objectives that elicit higher levels of thought than the mere memory or knowledge level; he may also begin to develop objectives dealing with values and attitudes.

9. If each objective clearly indicates a desired learning behavior, the teacher need not fear the "technical" criticisms of others.

EXAMINING THE PERFORMANCE OBJECTIVE

I. Basic design of the behavioral objective
   A. Measurable verb
   B. Behavior (or performance) of the student
   C. Conditions
   D. Criterion or standard

II. Location in teaching-learning design (as it relates to a learning package)
   A. Goal—general and broad
      1. General instructional objective—deals with concepts, understanding, etc.

       a. Performance objective
       b. Performance objective
       c. Performance objective
   2. General instructional objective
       a. Performance objective
       b. Performance objective
       c. Performance objective

III. Characteristics of a good performance objective

1. Demonstrates validity in relation to the basic goals and direction of the course
2. Identifies measurable behavior—if it is not measurable or observable, it is not behavioral, not clear
3. Possesses content generality (see Popham)—is not merely written as a test item
4. Is not limited to the knowledge level—ascend the academic scale; see Bloom taxonomy
5. Measures, where possible, values and attitudes—see Krathwohl taxonomy (affective domain)
6. Maintains balance between "process" and product in education
   a. Process oriented—does the student know how to go about learning?
   b. Product oriented—how much did the student learn; at what level can he perform?

HOW TO DEVELOP LEARNING PACKAGES

LEARNING PACKAGES

Definition: A learning package consists of one significant segment of the course being taught; it may be equivalent to a chapter, a unit, or that segment of a course or discipline containing a major concept or family of concepts. Different courses or subject areas may vary in their number of learning packages.

    Value: The use of learning packages is of special help to the teacher who seeks to (1) allow each student to learn at his optimum rate and manner, (2) give individual assistance to students, and (3) allow students choices in their learning experiences.

    Names: Learning packages have been given various names; a few of these are Unit Paks, learning activities packages (LAPs), levels, and learning packages.

    The following sections are designed to assist teachers with the task of developing learning packages. The "generations" referred to on the following pages are merely to help the teacher see that his initial learning packages may need to be refined and improved as time goes on. This is true, of course, for all teaching procedures.

REFINING AND IMPROVING THE LEARNING PACKAGE

The steps in developing learning packages may be viewed as follows:

    First Generation Learning Package: This is the basic learning package containing the elements essential to individualized learning.

Second Generation Learning Package: In the second generation learning package the teacher may introduce a variety of options; these options might include additional forms of the pretest and post-test. Options in learning activities also may be introduced.

Third Generation Learning Package: At this point the instructor should endeavor to include enough variety in each aspect of the learning package to meet the varied needs and abilities of all students. (Examples of first, second, and third generation package items are on following pages.)

Suggested Procedure: The teacher should start with a first generation learning package during the first year or during his early experiences with individualized instruction. As time allows, the teacher may edit, add to, and revise the first generation learning package, thus developing second and third generation learning packages.

FIRST-GENERATION LEARNING PACKAGE

Goal: The major task or goal (of the unit, chapter, or level) must be identified. Teacher and students must have a sense of direction and a definite idea of what is to be accomplished.

Performance Objectives (behavioral): Performance objectives are the steps which move the learner toward the goal. Each objective is written in terms of what the learner will be able to do; it is to be an activity which is measurable or observable.

Pretest: A pretest is given to determine the student's readiness and/or his present needs or capabilities as they relate to the objectives of the learning package.

Prescription: Assignments are based on the pretests. Each student is assigned to those learning experiences he needs to enable him to reach the objectives of the learning package.

Instruction: Emphasis is placed upon setting up appropriate learning experiences for individual students. The instructor needs to view the matter of group sizes and the time element as two areas in which to be flexible if provision is to be made for individual student needs.

Post-Test: The post-test determines the student's readiness to go on to the next learning package. The test must be based on the requirements contained in the performance objectives.

Exit or Recycle: Having completed the requirements of the learning package, the student exits and goes on to the next learning package. Should he not reach the standards outlined, he is recycled into the learning package in which he has been studying.

SECOND-GENERATION LEARNING PACKAGE

Performance Objectives: Refine as needed.

Pretest: Develop options, perhaps called Forms A, B, C, and so forth.

Prescription: Refine optional assignments. Add to existing materials and learning sources. Additions may include film strips, additional books, cassettes, and so forth.

Instruction: Add teaching strategies that may be more effective for individual students. Two important additions should be provided in most subject areas:

1. Interaction experiences: Students should be given opportunities to interact—to share their learning experiences with the instructor and with other students. When interaction is omitted individualized learning is similar to correspondence work.
2. Maintenance: Provision should be made for appropriate practice, drill, and review to enable students to maintain the required skills or learning. Extinction, or loss of skills or knowledge, takes place when periodic practice and review are not provided.

Post-Test: Develop options. Pretests and post-tests could be used interchangeably.

THIRD-GENERATION LEARNING PACKAGE

Performance objectives: Further refinement may include the development of objectives eliciting higher levels of thought (see Bloom's taxonomy) and objectives relating to attitudes and values (see Krathwohl's taxonomy).

Pretest: The instructor may refine the assessment process by including other means of determining student readiness; standardized tests, student records, and conferences may contribute to this more comprehensive assessment process.

Prescription: The instructor may continue to refine individualized assignments.

Instruction: Among the additional teaching strategies that may be added are:

1. Audio-tutorial teaching methods: The approach here may involve the coordinated use of objectives, texts, classroom instruction, and cassette tapes.
2. Quest opportunities: Quest opportunities involve more extended learning opportunities for skilled students and/or students having special interests in the topic of the learning package.
3. Careers: The instructor should endeavor to relate the students' learning experiences to the world of work and to career opportunities. The Union Conference and conferences will provide assistance in this area.

Post-Test: Continue the development of option tests. The instructor may wish to include oral examinations, evaluation of student projects, and so forth to determine students' progress.

A SUMMARY OF THE LEARNING PACKAGE CYCLE

The following are basic procedures involved in the learning package.

1. **Identifying Goals and Objectives.**
2. **Assessment:** Assessment of student readiness may be accomplished by a combination of activities such as pretesting, interviewing, analyzing achievement tests, and so forth. Assessment is often referred to as preassessment or diagnosis.
3. **Prescription:** Prescription is almost synonymous with "assignments." The basic difference is that "prescription" involves the issuing of assignments based upon a previous assessment and upon the student's needs.
4. **Instruction:** Instruction is the teacher's role in the student's learning experience. The method of instruction should be that which is most appropriate to the learner's needs and most suitable to the subject being taught.
5. **Evaluation:** Evaluation of student progress takes place throughout the learning experience; however, in the learning package special emphasis is placed on the pretest (which is part of the original assessment of student readiness) and on the post-test. The post-test measures the student's readiness to progress to the next learning package.
6. **Exit:** Exit takes place when the student's performance reaches the standards within the particular package. Having reached the required standards, the student is allowed to "exit" and to go on to the next learning package.
7. **Recycle:** Should a student fail to reach the standards required, he is recycled into the learning experiences within the learning package. Efforts should be made to give the learner different learning materials and experiences; this should be done to relieve boredom and to facilitate his reaching the required standards.

HOW TO REPORT PUPIL PROGRESS

A. Follow two principles of measurement:
    1. Measure the student's individual progress regardless of how he compares with others (criterion-referenced measurement).
    2. Measure the student's position as it relates to others (norm-referenced measurement).
    3. Place greater emphasis on criterion-referenced measurement than on norm-referenced measurement.
B. The report form should include:
    1. Spaces indicating the level at which a student started in a subject.
    2. Spaces indicating the student's current level of achievement.
    3. A description of the skills or understanding required at the level reached.
    4. Symbols identifying the amount of effort the student has put into the learning experience.

BIBLIOGRAPHY

Alexander, William M. THE CHANGING HIGH SCHOOL CURRICULUM, 2nd. ed. New York: Holt, Rinehart and Winston, 1972.

"Alternative Public Schools: What Are They?" NATIONAL ASSOCIATION OF SECONDARY SCHOOL PRINCIPALS BULLETIN, September 1973, p. 7.

Anthonita, M. "The Ungraded Primary: An Adventure in Achievement." CATHOLIC SCHOOL JOURNAL, March 1967, pp. 68–70.

Anthony, Albert S. "Twenty Unprinciples for Successful Innovation." CLEARING HOUSE 46(1971): 32–34.

Armstrong, Harold R. TEACHING PERFORMANCE EVALUATION. Worthington, Ohio: School Management Institute, 1972.

Baker, Gail L., and Goldberg, Isadore. "The Individualized Learning System." EDUCATIONAL LEADERSHIP 27(1970): 775–780.

Bennis, Warren G.; Benne, Kenneth D.; and Chin, Robert. THE PLANNING OF CHANGE, 2nd ed. New York: Holt, Rinehart and Winston, 1969.

Bethune, Paul. "The Nova Plan for Individualized Learning." SCIENCE TEACHER 33(1966): 55–57.

Blackwood, Andrew. THE PROTESTANT PULPIT. New York: Abingdon-Cokesbury Press, 1947.

Blake, Howard E., and McPherson, Ann W. "Individualized Instruction—Where are We?" EDUCATIONAL TECHNOLOGY 9(1969): 64–65.

Bloom, Benjamin S., ed. TAXONOMY OF EDUCATIONAL OBJECTIVES: THE COGNITIVE DOMAIN. New York: McKay, 1956.

Boston, Robert E., and Wendt, Marilynn S. "Nongrading an Entire System." MICHIGAN EDUCATIONAL JOURNAL 43(1966): 21–22.

Branan, Karen. "I Get a Very Different Feeling in That Class . . ." SCHOLASTIC TEACHER, 3 May 1971, pp. 8–10.

Bremer, Anne, and Bremer, John. OPEN EDUCATION: A BEGINNING. New York: Holt, Rinehart and Winston, 1972.

Brodinsky, Ben, ed. "Grading and Reporting." CURRENT TRENDS IN SCHOOL POLICIES AND PROGRAMS, October 1972.

Brody, Erness Bright. "Achievement of First- and Second-Year Pupils in Graded and Nongraded Classrooms." THE ELEMENTARY SCHOOL JOURNAL 70(1970): 391–394.

Brown, B. Frank. THE APPROPRIATE PLACEMENT SCHOOL: A SOPHISTICATED NONGRADED CURRICULUM. West Nyack, N.Y.: Parker Publishing Company, 1965.

Brown, George Isaac. HUMAN TEACHING FOR HUMAN LEARNING. New York: Viking, 1971.

Brown, William R. "EPIC . . . An Innovative Curricular Model." SCIENCE TEACHER 37(1970): 65–68.

Bruner, Jerome S. ON KNOWING. Forge Village, Mass.: Murray Printing Company, 1962.

Bruner, Jerome S. TOWARD A THEORY OF INSTRUCTION. Cambridge, Mass.: Belknap Press, 1966.

Burke, Daniel J. "Variables To Be Considered in Planning for Educational Change." Los Angeles: Center for Excellence in Education, School of Education, University of Southern California, n.d.

Bushnell, David S., and Rappaport, Donald. PLANNED CHANGE IN EDUCATION: A SYSTEMS APPROACH. New York: Harcourt Brace Jovanovich, 1971.

Casavis, James N. "Non-Gradedness: A Formula for Change." NEW YORK STATE EDUCATION, December 1969, pp. 22–23.

Champlin, John R. "A Spirit in Search of Substance: Another View of Nongradedness." NEW YORK STATE EDUCATION, May 1969, p. 18.

Cirone, Claire, and Emerson, Patricia. "A Continuous Progress Program." NEW YORK STATE EDUCATION, January 1966, p. 19.

Clark, Donald C., and Clark, Sally N. "Preparation of the Staff for Utilizing the Pontoon Transitional Design." Los Angeles: Center for Excellence in Education, School of Education, University of Southern California, n.d.

Clark, Leonard H., et al. THE AMERICAN SECONDARY SCHOOL CURRICULUM, 2nd ed. New York: Macmillan, 1972.

Dunn, Rita, and Dunn, Kenneth. PRACTICAL APPROACHES TO INDIVIDUALIZING INSTRUCTION. West Nyack, N.Y.: Parker Publishing Company, 1972.

Eble, Kenneth E. A PERFECT EDUCATION. New York: Macmillan, 1966.

"Evaluating New Strategies in Teaching and Learning." JOURNAL OF SECONDARY EDUCATION 45(1970): 320–325.

Fantini, Mario. "Education by Choice." NATIONAL ASSOCIATION OF SECONDARY SCHOOL PRINCIPALS BULLETIN, November 1973, pp. 10–19.

Featherstone, Joseph. SCHOOLS WHERE CHILDREN LEARN. New York: Liveright, 1971.

Finkelstein, Leonard B. "Implementation: Essentials for Success." NATIONAL ASSOCIATION OF SECONDARY SCHOOL PRINCIPALS BULLETIN, November 1973, pp. 39–41.

Ford, James E. "Cassville Individualizes Teaching." SCHOOL AND COMMUNITY 55(1969): 15.

Full, Harold. CONTROVERSY IN AMERICAN EDUCATION, 2nd ed. New York: Macmillan, 1972.

Georgiades, William. "The Pontoon Transitional Design for Curriculum Change." Los Angeles: Center for Excellence in Education, School of Education, University of Southern California, n.d.

Georgiades, William, and Udinsky, B.F. "Selected Bibliography on Staff Utilization, Fall, 1974." Los Angeles: Center for Excellence in Education, School of Education, University of Southern California, n.d.

Georgiades, William, and Clark, Donald C., eds. MODELS FOR INDIVIDUALIZED INSTRUCTION. New York: MSS Information Corp., 1974.

Georgiades, William, ed. "Individualizing Instruction." THRUST, April 1973, pp. 1–47.

Gerhard, Muriel. EFFECTIVE TEACHING STRATEGIES WITH THE BEHAVIORAL OUTCOMES APPROACH. West Nyack, N.Y.: Parker Publishing Company, 1971.

Glasser, William. SCHOOLS WITHOUT FAILURE. New York: Harper & Row, 1969.

Goodlad, John I. "The Nongraded School." THE NATIONAL ELEMENTARY PRINCIPAL 50(1970): 24–27.

Goodlad, John I., and Anderson, Robert. THE NON-GRADED ELEMENTARY SCHOOL, rev. ed. New York: Harcourt, Brace & World, 1963.

Goodlad, John I.; Klein, Frances; et al. BEHIND THE CLASSROOM DOOR. Worthington, Ohio: Charles A. Jones, 1970.

Gordon, William M.; Whitesell, Philip A.; and Joy, Donald. "ImPALLA—A New Approach to Secondary School Language Arts." ENGLISH JOURNAL 59(1970): 534–539.

Gray, Russell Dent, III. "The Implementation of Pontooning Within Elementary Schools." Los Angeles: Center for Excellence in Education, School of Education, University of Southern California, n.d.

Greenberg, James D., and Rough, Robert E. "A Visit to the 'School Without Walls': Two Impressions." PHI DELTA KAPPAN 51(1970): 480–484.

Gronlund, Norman E. STATING BEHAVIORAL OBJECTIVES FOR CLASSROOM INSTRUCTION. New York: Macmillan, 1970.

Halbert, T. D., and Adamac, M. "The Unit-Pak: A Practical Approach to Individualization." Monograph No. 6. Calgary, Alberta: Division of Continuing Education, University of Calgary, 1972.

Harrow, Anita J. A TAXONOMY OF THE PSYCHOMOTOR DOMAIN. New York: McKay, 1972.

Havelock, Ronald G. A GUIDE TO INNOVATION IN EDUCATION. Ann Arbor, Mich.: Center for Research on Utilization of Scientific Knowledge, Institute for Social Research, 1970.

Hearn, Norman E. "The Where, When and How of Trying Innovations." PHI DELTA KAPPAN 53(1972): 358–362, 374.

Hertzberg, Alvin, and Stone, Edward. SCHOOLS ARE FOR CHILDREN. New York: Schocken Books, 1971.

Hickey, M. E. "Evaluation in Alternative Education." NATIONAL ASSOCIATION OF SECONDARY SCHOOL PRINCIPALS BULLETIN, November 1973, pp. 103–109.

Hillson, Maurie, and Bongo, Joseph. CONTINUOUS PROGRESS EDUCATION, A PRACTICAL APPROACH. Palo Alto, Calif.: Science Research Associates, 1971.

Hillson, Maurie, and Hyman, Ronald T. CHANGE AND INNOVATION IN ELEMENTARY AND SECONDARY ORGANIZATION. New York: Holt, Rinehart and Winston, 1971.

Holder, Herbert R. "Scheduling for Pontooning." Los Angeles: Center for Excellence in Education, School of Education, University of Southern California, n.d.

Holt, John. HOW CHILDREN LEARN. New York: Pitman, 1967.

Howard, Eugene R. "Developing Sequential Learning Materials." NATIONAL ASSOCIATION OF SECONDARY SCHOOL PRINCIPALS BULLETIN, May 1970, pp. 159–168.

Howell, Bruce. "Designing and Implementing Alternative Schools." NATIONAL ASSOCIATION OF SECONDARY SCHOOL PRINCIPALS BULLETIN, November 1973, pp. 32–38.

Howes, Virgil M. INDIVIDUALIZATION OF INSTRUCTION. New York: Macmillan, 1970.

Hunter, Madeline. "Tailor Your Teaching to Individualized Instruction." INSTRUCTION 79(1970): 53–63.

"Individualized Education: An Essential Ingredient in Individualized Learning." NATIONAL ASSOCIATION OF SECONDARY SCHOOL PRINCIPALS BULLETIN, May 1974, pp. 57–72.

"Innovations—What Is Expected? Probing the Concept Theoretically and Practically." NATIONAL ASSOCIATION OF SECONDARY SCHOOL PRINCIPALS BULLETIN, February 1973, pp. 1–91.

Jennings, Wayne. "Implementing Options: The Imperatives." NATIONAL ASSOCIATION OF SECONDARY SCHOOL PRINCIPALS BULLETIN, November 1973, pp. 26–31.

Jones, Loren S., and Jones, Virginia. "Creating Opportunities for Individual Growth." NATIONAL ASSOCIATION OF SECONDARY SCHOOL PRINCIPALS BULLETIN, February 1972, pp. 38–45.

Kapfer, Philip G., and Ovard, Glen F. PREPARING AND USING INDIVIDUALIZED LEARNING PACKAGES FOR UNGRADED, CONTINUOUS PROGRESS EDUCATION. Englewood Cliffs, N.J.: Educational Technology Publications, 1971.

Kibler, Robert J., et al. BEHAVIORAL OBJECTIVES AND INSTRUCTION. Boston: Allyn & Bacon, 1970.

Kirschenbaum, Howard; Simon, Sidney B.; and Napier, Rodney W. WAD-JA-GET? New York: Hart Publishing Company, 1971.

Krathwohl, David R., ed. TAXONOMY OF EDUCATIONAL OBJECTIVES: AFFECTIVE DOMAIN. New York: McKay, 1968.

Leonard, George B. EDUCATION AND ECSTASY. New York: Delacorte Press, 1968.

Lewis, C. S. AN EXPERIMENT IN CRITICISM. New York: Cambridge University Press, 1969.

Lieberman, Myron, et al. "An Overview of Accountability." PHI DELTA KAPPAN 52(1970): 194–243.

Mager, Robert F. GOAL ANALYSIS. Belmont, Calif.: Fearon Publishers, 1972.

Mager, Robert F. PREPARING INSTRUCTIONAL OBJECTIVES. Palo Alto, Calif.: Fearon Publishers, 1962.

Mager, Robert F., and Pipe, Peter. ANALYZING PERFORMANCE PROBLEMS, OR YOU REALLY OUGHTA WANNA. Belmont, Calif.: Fearon Publishers, 1970.

Massialas, Bryon G., and Zevin, Jack. CREATIVE ENCOUNTERS IN THE CLASSROOM. New York: Wiley, 1967.

McClosky, Mildred G., ed. TEACHING STRATEGIES AND CLASSROOM REALITIES. Englewood Cliffs, N.J.: Prentice-Hall, 1971.

McKinney, William D., and Partin, Jack L. "Personalized Instruction: Strategy for Change." Los Angeles: Center for Excellence in Education, School of Education, University of Southern California, n.d.

McNeil, John D. TOWARD ACCOUNTABLE TEACHERS. New York: Holt, Rinehart and Winston, 1971.

Miles, Matthew B., ed. INNOVATION IN EDUCATION. New York: Teachers College Press, 1964.

Morris, John E. "Accountability: Watchword for the 70's." CLEARING HOUSE 45(1971): 323–328.

Murphy, Gardner. "Motivation: The Key to Changing Educational Times." EDUCATION DIGEST 36(1971): 39–42.

Nichols, Roy D., Jr., and Cleare, Mary Jane. "Alternative or a Copout?" NATIONAL ASSOCIATION OF SECONDARY SCHOOL PRINCIPALS BULLETIN, November 1973, pp. 20–25.

Olivero, James L. "The Meaning and Application of Differentiated Staffing in Teaching." PHI DELTA KAPPAN 51(1970): 36–40.

Olivero, James L., and Buffie, Edward G., eds. EDUCATIONAL MANPOWER. Bloomington: Indiana University Press, 1970.

Oppenheimer, Martin. "Successful and Unsuccessful Change in Two Educational Settings." THE JOURNAL OF GENERAL EDUCATION 22(1970): 175–185.

Ovard, Glen F. "Effects on Students Moving from an Individualized Continuous Progress School to a More Traditional School." NATIONAL ASSOCIATION OF SECONDARY SCHOOL PRINCIPALS BULLETIN, November 1973, pp. 73–79.

Ovard, Glen F. "The Practitioner's Guide to Research: Effects on Students." NATIONAL ASSOCIATION OF SECONDARY SCHOOLS BULLETIN, November 1973, pp. 73–79.

Paskal, Dolores, and Miller, William C. "Can Options Work in Smaller School Districts?" NATIONAL ASSOCIATION OF SECONDARY SCHOOL PRINCIPALS BULLETIN, November 1973, pp. 47–54.

Plowman, Paul D. BEHAVIORAL OBJECTIVES: TEACHER SUCCESS THROUGH STUDENT PERFORMANCE. Chicago: Science Research Associates, 1971.

Popham, W. James. "The Instructional Objectives Exchange: New Support for Criterion-Referenced Instruction." PHI DELTA KAPPAN 51(1970): 174–175.

Popham, W. James. THE TEACHER-EMPIRICIST. Los Angeles: Tinnon-Brown, 1970.

Popham, W. James, and Baker, Eva I. ESTABLISHING INSTRUCTIONAL GOALS. Englewood Cliffs, N.J.: 1970.

Popham, W. James, and Baker, Eva I. EXPANDING DIMENSIONS OF INSTRUCTIONAL OBJECTIVES. Englewood Cliffs, N.J.: Prentice-Hall, 1970.

Popham, W. James, and Baker, Eva I. PLANNING INSTRUCTIONAL OBJECTIVES. Englewood Cliffs, N.J.: Prentice-Hall, 1970.

Postman, Neil, and Weingartner, Charles. TEACHING AS A SUBVERSIVE ACTIVITY. New York: Delacorte Press, 1969.

Pusey, Nathan. THE AGE OF THE SCHOLAR. New York: Harper Torchbooks, 1963.

Rogers, Carl R. FREEDOM TO LEARN. Columbus, Ohio: Merrill, 1969.

Saroson, Seymour B. THE CULTURE OF THE SCHOOL AND THE PROBLEM OF CHANGE. Boston: Allyn & Bacon, 1971.

Schaefer, Robert J. THE SCHOOL AS A CENTER OF INQUIRY. New York: Harper & Row, 1967.

"School Is Not a Place but an Activity." MEDIA AND METHODS 6(1970): 30.

SCHOOLS FOR THE 70'S AND BEYOND: A CALL TO ACTION. Center for the Study of Instruction, National Education Association, Main Report, 1971.

Sciara, Frank J., and Jantz, Richard K. ACCOUNTABILITY IN AMERICAN EDUCATION. Boston: Allyn & Bacon, 1972.

Scobey, M. M., and Graham, Grace, eds. TO NURTURE HUMANENESS. 1970 ASCD Yearbook.

Shurtleff, Ray F. "Administrative Problems? Cambridge Pilot School." NATIONAL ASSOCIATION OF SECONDARY SCHOOL PRINCIPALS BULLETIN, November 1973, pp. 76–82.

Silberman, Charles E. CRISIS IN THE CLASSROOM. New York: Random House, 1970.

Silberman, Charles E., ed. THE OPEN CLASSROOM READER. New York: Vintage Books, 1973.

Simon, Sidney B., et al. VALUES CLARIFICATION. New York: Hart, 1972.

Skinner, B. F. BEYOND FREEDOM AND DIGNITY. New York: Knopf, 1971.

Skinner, B. F. WALDEN TWO. New York: Macmillan, 1948.

Smith, Louis M., and Keith, Pat M. ANATOMY OF EDUCATIONAL INNOVATION. New York: Wiley, 1971.

Snow, C. P. THE TWO CULTURES AND A SECOND LOOK. New York: Cambridge University Press, 1959.

Spencer, Ralph. "In Defense of Administrivia." NATIONAL ASSOCIATION OF SECONDARY SCHOOL PRINCIPALS BULLETIN, November 1970, pp. 90–94.

Stocker, Joseph, and Wilson, Donald F. "Accountability and the Classroom Teacher." TODAY'S EDUCATION 60(1971): 41–56.

Trump, J. Lloyd. "Changes Needed for Further Improvement of Secondary Education." NATIONAL ASSOCIATION OF SECONDARY SCHOOL PRINCIPALS BULLETIN, January 1969, pp. 117–133.

Trump, J. Lloyd. "On Humanizing Schools: Point of View and Basic Issues." NATIONAL ASSOCIATION OF SECONDARY SCHOOL PRINCIPALS BULLETIN, February 1972, pp. 9–16.

Trump, J. Lloyd, and Georgiades, William. "Doing Better with What You Have—NASSP Model Schools Project." NATIONAL ASSOCIATION OF SECONDARY SCHOOL PRINCIPALS BULLETIN, May 1970, pp. 106–133.

Trump, J. Lloyd, and Georgiades, William. "Factors That Facilitate and Limit Change—From the Vantage of the NASSP Model Schools Project." NATIONAL ASSOCIATION OF SECONDARY SCHOOL PRINCIPALS BULLETIN, May 1973, pp. 93–102.

Trump, J. Lloyd, and Georgiades, William. "How To Evaluate the Quality of Educational Programs." NATIONAL ASSOCIATION OF SECONDARY SCHOOL PRINCIPALS BULLETIN, May 1975, pp. 99–103.

Trump, J. Lloyd, and Georgiades, William. "The NASSP Model Schools Action Program." NATIONAL ASSOCIATION OF SECONDARY SCHOOL PRINCIPALS BULLETIN, May 1972, pp. 116–126.

Trump, J. Lloyd, and Georgiades, William. "Which Elements of School Programs Are Easier To Change and Which Are Most Difficult—And Why?" NATIONAL ASSOCIATION OF SECONDARY SCHOOL PRINCIPALS BULLETIN, May 1971, pp. 54–68.

Trump, J. Lloyd, and Miller, Delmas F. SECONDARY SCHOOL CURRICULUM IMPROVEMENT, 2nd ed. Boston: Allyn & Bacon, 1973.

Turnbull, William W. "The Uses of Measurement in Individualized Education." NATIONAL ASSOCIATION OF SECONDARY SCHOOL PRINCIPALS BULLETIN, May 1970, pp. 80–87.

Tyler, Ralph W. BASIC PRINCIPLES OF CURRICULUM AND INSTRUCTION. Chicago: University of Chicago Press, 1950.

Udinsky, B. Flavian, ed. "Change Efforts for the 70's." JOURNAL OF SECONDARY EDUCATION 46(1971): 4.

Umans, Shelley. "Options in Large School Districts." NATIONAL ASSOCIATION OF SECONDARY SCHOOL PRINCIPALS BULLETIN, November 1973, pp. 42–46.

Van Til, William, ed. CURRICULUM: QUEST FOR RELEVANCE. Boston: Houghton Mifflin, 1971.

Vaughan, Maury S. "Change in Education: The New and the Not So New." SCHOOL & SOCIETY, October 1971, pp. 341–344.

Vernon, Walter M. MOTIVATING CHILDREN. New York: Holt, Rinehart and Winston, 1972.

Von Haden, Herbert I., and King, Jean Marie. INNOVATIONS IN EDUCATION: THEIR PROS AND CONS. Worthington, Ohio: Charles A. Jones, 1971.

Weigand, James E., ed. DEVELOPING TEACHER COMPETENCIES. Englewood Cliffs, N.J.: Prentice-Hall, 1971.

Weinstein, Gerald, and Fantini, Mario. TOWARD HUMANISTIC EDUCATION: A CURRICULUM OF AFFECT. New York: Praeger, 1970.

Wilmoth, Juanita, and Ehn, Willard. "The Inflexibility of Flexible Modular Scheduling." EDUCATIONAL LEADERSHIP 27(1970): 727–731.

ADDRESSES

National Association of Secondary School Principals
1904 Association Drive
Reston, Virginia 22091

University of Texas at Austin
Austin, Texas 78712

General Programmed Teaching
Quail Hill
San Rafael, CA 94903

Institute for the Development of Education Activities (IDEA)
5335 Far Hills Ave.
Dayton, Ohio 45429

Educational Technology Audio Tape Cassettes
140 Sylvan Ave.
Englewood Cliffs, N.J. 07632

MEDIA RESOURCES

"And No Bells Ring." Washington, D.C.: NASSP. A two-part film depicting the NASSP's ideas on staff utilization. The two half-hour films show teaching teams, large-group instruction, small-group instruction, independent study, and small discussion groups. May be rented from the National Association of Secondary School Principals (NASSP).

"And Now What?" Washington, D.C.: NASSP, 1969. With the many efforts at innovation, this NASSP release attempts to look ahead at the school, its program, and the future services it must provide for youth.

"Answers and Questions." Washington, D.C.: NASSP, 1968. 16mm, color, sound (24 minutes). This film is a must for all educators interested in improving teaching-learning environments. It asks questions and provides some answers; but more importantly, it is highly stimulating and thought provoking. It is a "tell it like it is" film with excellent opportunities for student participation.

"Can Individualization Work in Your School System?" SPF, 1965. 16mm,

color, sound (41 minutes). Dr. John Goodland, Professor of Education at UCLA, presents evidence to indicate that no other approach to childhood education will work as well as individualization. He first analyzes some of the individual differences among learners that make personalized instruction necessary. His lecture then goes into the kind of changes in school organization curriculum and methods of teaching that may be required in a school system to provide individual instruction for each child in a group situation. May be rented from the University of Texas at Austin.

"Continuous Progress Learning." Dayton, Ohio: IDEA. 16mm, color, sound (22 minutes). What is a spiral curriculum? How effective is it? Using the Sea Mills Infant School in Bristol, England, as a starting point, this teacher-training film explores the principle that children can learn at varying speeds and in varying ways. They also benefit most from a curriculum of continuous learning that is paced to the individual child's ability and desire to learn. May be rented or purchased from the

Institute for the Development of Education Activities (IDEA).

"Designing Effective Instruction." Palo Alto, Calif.: General Programmed Teaching. A comprehensive program of teacher in-service training in individualization. The first five units, each with filmstrip, cassette, and manual, deal with basic principles; general goals, affective objectives, and cognitive objectives; components of an objective; classification of objectives; and criterion tests. Other more advanced specialized units are also available. An excellent resource.

Educational Technology Audio Tape Cassettes. Englewood Cliffs, N.J.: Educational Technology. A series of cassettes recommended for personal use and for preservice and in-service training. Titles now available include: "An Introduction to Educational Technology" (12 cassettes); "Varied Aspects of Educational Technology" (20 cassettes); and "Educational Technology in Practice" (4 cassettes). May be ordered individually or as complete sets.

"Focus on Change." Washington, D.C.: NASSP, 1962. A filmstrip relating the findings and recommendations of the Commission on Experimental Study of Staff Utilization in the Secondary School. A recorded narration is given by Howard K. Smith.

"Focus on the Individual: A Leadership Responsibility." Washington, D.C.: NASSP, 1965. A color filmstrip with accompanying 28-minute narration. A printed copy of the script (developed by J. Lloyd Trump and Lois Karask) is included.

"The Improbable Form of Master Sturm — The Nongraded High School." Dayton, Ohio: IDEA. 16mm, color, sound (13 minutes). This film acquaints the viewer with the highlights of nongradedness and furnishes persons interested in the concept with insight into its many ramifications. Individual rather than group needs are shown as important aspects of the nongraded curriculum. The basic premise is that, with proper guidance, the individual — slow, average, or superior — can transform his school experience into one of inquiry, curiosity, and problem solving. Can be rented or purchased.

"Individual Motivation and Behavior." NET. 16mm, black and white (30 minutes). This film explores with individuals of a demonstration group the basis for their own actions within the group. From the Dynamics of Leadership Series. May be rented for $5.40 from the University of Texas at Austin.

"I Walk Away in the Rain." HRAW, 1969. 16mm, color, sound (11 minutes). This film, from the Critical Moments in Teaching Series, explores the problem of motivating a highly capable adolescent who puts forth minimal effort in schoolwork. May be rented from the University of Texas at Austin.

"Learning Through Inquiry." Dayton, Ohio: IDEA. 16mm, color, sound (22 minutes). Are there any different approaches to old problems? This film attempts to show some. The teacher's function is changed from dispenser of facts to stimulator of interest and imagination. Students are placed into four-member groups to attack questions as a team. The film, focusing on one of these groups of youngsters, presents an innovative technique that improves learning and costs little to utilize. May be rented for $12.50 or purchased for $225.00.

"Make a Mighty Reach." IDEA Corporation. A film that examines modern innovation efforts in teaching. Focusing on both elementary and secondary education, the film encourages greater efforts in making education relevant to all students.

"More Different Than Alike." NEA, 1967. 16mm, color, sound (30 minutes). Depicts some unique and creative techniques that provide for individual learning differences. The film shows a data processing system used to compare the progress each student is making with the progress he **should** be making. It also covers a special school for the slow learner, a learning center in which high school students have access to the latest materials and technology for self-instruction, a program of student-planned work schedules and learning projects, and a "helpmobile" for in-service education. May be rented from the University of Texas at Austin.

"Motivation Theory for Teachers, Part II: Translating Theory into Classroom Practice." SPF, 1969. 16mm, color, sound (28 minutes). How to get Johnny's intellectual motor started —

a discussion of the six variables that are subject to control by the teacher and that influence motivation. After viewing the film, a teacher should be able to apply motivation theory in daily classroom practice. May be rented for $6.00 from the University of Texas at Austin.

"New Options for Learning — Urban Education." Dayton, Ohio: IDEA. 16 mm, color, sound (22 minutes). This film deals with the changes taking place in our city schools. Because city schools are so desperately in need of help, they are willing to try some of the most striking changes that American education has seen. "New Options for Learning" is a portrayal of novel approaches to education that are emanating from the inner city. It is the story of the quiet battles being fought and the small victories being won in unorthodox learning environments designed to meet the different needs and learning styles of children. This film relates a small, scattered, but irreversible start. May be rented for $12.50 or purchased for $225.00.

"No Reason to Stay." New York: McGraw-Hill. This movie from the Film Board of Canada relates the story of an intelligent youth who rebelled against the rigidity of the school system and dropped out. His story conveys meaningful reasons to remain in school, but it stresses the necessity of challenging students through the educational process.

"The Open Laboratory." STNFRD, 1966. 16mm, color, sound (28 minutes). Dr. Dwight Allen, Professor of Education at Stanford University, describes laboratories that provide for individualization and an expanded range of instructional alternatives based on performance criteria. This film is from the Innovations in Education Series. May be rented for $7.50 from the University of Texas at Austin.

"Performance Curriculum I: Issues in Innovation." STNFRD, 1967. 16mm, color, sound (28 minutes). Dr. Dwight Allen discusses the problems and issues of innovation, emphasizing curriculum and educational change. This film is from the Innovations in Education Series. May be rented for $7.50 from the University of Texas at Austin.

"Performance Curriculum II: Issues in Organization." STNFRD, 1966. 16mm, color, sound (28 minutes). Dr. Dwight Allen considers a flexible model for organizational innovation in this film from the Innovations in Education Series. May be rented for $7.50 from the University of Texas at Austin.

"Preparing Projected Materials." VEF, 1965. 16mm, color, sound (15 minutes). This film illustrates the growth of the audio-visual field by contrasting the old magic lantern with modern projection materials. It also discusses the use of projectors, 2'' by 2'' format cameras, Polaroid copying stands, and Thermofax copiers. May be rented for $6.00 from the University of Texas at Austin.

"The Present is Prologue." Washington, D.C.: NASSP, 1966. This film shows the current trends in education, focusing on the idea that what is now being attempted in terms of innovation is simply a beginning or foundation for what must come in years ahead.

Project Talent. California State Department of Education. Each of these fourteen films is approximately 30 minutes in length. Some, but not all, deal with Bloom's taxonomy of educational objectives. They are distributed by Acme Film & Video-Tape Laboratories, 1611 North Highland Avenue, Hollywood, California 90038, Attention: Patricia Licini.

"The Quiet Revolution." NEA, 1967. 16mm, color, sound (28 minutes). This film depicts a variety of staffing patterns in schools that have initiated team teaching, nongraded elementary programs, flexible scheduling, and other innovations. May be rented for $7.00 from the University of Texas at Austin.

"Rationale of the Model Schools Project." Washington, D.C.: NASSP. Twenty-seven slides and audio tapes prepared by J. Lloyd Trump, Director of the NASSP Model Schools Project, presenting an overview of the program and how to obtain information about it.

"Resource Center." UMINN, 1948. 16mm, color, sound (28 minutes). Dr. Dwight Allen presents the functions and uses of resource centers for students in various academic areas and mentions the operation, staffing, and administration of such centers. This film is from the Innovations in Education Series. May be rented for $7.50 from the University of Texas at Austin.

"Rx for Learning." HEW-UP, 1969. 16mm, color, sound (29 minutes). This film was produced after the Individually Prescribed Instruction Program had been in operation and under study for several semesters. It shows the learning continuum, its constant evaluation and change where necessary, and how it is applied to different achievement levels. Progress is being recorded for future evaluation and comparison with other students both in and out of the program now and when they advance to junior and senior high school levels. May be rented for $6.00 from the University of Texas at Austin.

"Schools for Today and Tomorrow." AEGIS, 1967. 16mm, color, sound (15 minutes). This film shows new concepts in classroom design and teaching methods. May be rented for $4.00 from the University of Texas at Austin.

"Staff Meeting." Dayton, Ohio: IDEA. 16mm, black and white, sound (10 minutes). This film shows a staff discussion of problems involved in individualization, including grouping, inadequate materials, and working with children who have special learning problems. It features the principal, who assists teachers to think through their problems but who also cuts off discussion at some point when he feels strongly about the issue. The accompanying study guide discusses problem solving in staff meetings.

"The Strategies of Small-Group Learning." Dayton, Ohio: IDEA. 16mm, color, sound (26 minutes). Filmed on location in elementary, middle, and secondary schools across the country, this perusal of small-group learning transcends theory and illustrates practical application. The film is not intended to lecture teachers but to emphasize what other teachers are doing and how they achieve improved student performance with various types of small-group instruction. These techniques are amplified in the IDEA Occasional Paper "Learning in the Small Group," upon which the film is

based. Although the primary function of this film is teacher training, it is excellent for interested parents. May be rented for $13.50 or purchased for $250.00.

"The Teacher and Technology." USOE, 1967. 16mm, black and white (49 minutes). This film presents a series of pictorially documented programs that illustrate some of the ways in which technology is being used to meet the dual problems of masses of students and the need for individualized instruction. From the Communication Theory and the New Educational Media Series. May be rented for $3.50 from the University of Texas at Austin.

"Teacher to Teacher on Individualization, Part I: How To Get Individualization Started." SPF, 1969. 16mm, color, sound (28 minutes). Emphasizes the steps that need to be taken by the classroom teacher to individualize instruction. May be rented for $5.50 from the University of Texas at Austin.

"Teacher to Teacher on Individualization, Part II: How To Get Individualization Started — A Further Exploration." SPF, 1969. 16mm, color, sound (26 minutes). This film provides the viewer with specific illustrations of individualization and shows how a teacher analyzes each situation. May be rented for $5.50 from the University of Texas at Austin.

"Reinforcement Theory for Teachers, Part III: Translating Theory into Classroom Practice." SPF, 1969. 16mm, color, sound (28 minutes). How to increase behavior that advances learning and how to eliminate undesirable behavior — a discussion of positive reinforcement. After viewing this film, a teacher should understand the theory behind reward and punishment and should be able to apply reinforcement theory effectively in daily teaching. May be rented for $6.00 from the University of Texas at Austin.

"Tomorrow's Schools: Images and Plans." NASSP, 1972. 16mm, color, sound. Through clever use of graphics, J. Lloyd Trump and William Georgiades present the philosophical and psychological hypotheses that undergird the Model Schools Project. Through this film one is able to grasp the various concepts associated with the individualization of instruction:

changing roles of principals, teachers, students; continuous progress; use of facilities; and so forth.

"Understanding the Gifted." CF, 1965. 16mm, color, sound (33 minutes). This film uses student participants to point up four primary traits common to the gifted: ability to abstract and generalize, diverse and complex interests, the urge to create, and a well-defined sense of ethics and values. May be rented for $8.00 from the University of Texas at Austin.

Vicmet Audiotapes. Los Angeles: Vicmet Associates. This series of tapes, available in reel-to-reel or cassette form, deals with important issues in the field of instruction. These recordings can be used effectively in coordination with the Vicmet filmstrip-tape programs as well as with other in-service and preservice instructional sequences. Titles in the series are: "Behavioral Objectives Debate"; "Adapting to Student Differences"; "Criterion-Referenced Instruction"; "Conditions for Effective Learning"; "Objectives and Inservice Training"; "Teaching Performance Tests and Educational Accountability"; and "The Teacher and Accountability."

Vicmet Filmstrip-Tape Programs. Los Angeles: Vicmet Associates. All thirty programs in this series were prepared by W. James Popham and Eva Baker, Graduate School of Education, UCLA. Each of the programs includes an illustrated filmstrip, a taped narration, an instructor's manual, a statement of specific objectives accomplished by the program, reports of validation studies regarding the program's effectiveness, a sample copy of an optional response sheet, and a sample copy of a pre- and/or post-test.

"A Way of Learning — Project for Individualized Instruction." MPP, 1969. 16mm, color, sound (20 minutes). This is an overview of many different materials and media and how they may be utilized in individualization of instruction. The film includes team teaching, free movement of students, multilevel materials, and the extensive use of specialized staff. May be rented for $5.50 from the University of Texas at Austin.

"Why Are Team-Teaching and Non-Grading Important?" SPF, 1965. 16mm, black and white (49 minutes). Presents Dr. Goodland, who explains how team teaching and nongrading help to bridge the gap between the problems of school organization and individual learning differences. Number 3 in the How To Provide Personalized Education in a Public School Series. May be rented for $5.00 from the University of Texas at Austin.

"Why Visit Another School?" Dayton, Ohio: IDEA. 16mm, black and white, sound (15 minutes). This film shows a group of teachers discussing a recent visit to a highly individualized classroom. In this staff meeting they discuss and internalize what they saw and interpret it in relation to their own programs. The leadership role of the principal is featured. This is a real-life documentation of how one staff used visitation as a means of gathering data about changes they wished to bring about in their own program. A sidelight is the refutation of the notion that it is the "older teacher" who is resistant to change. The accompanying study guide suggests ways in which visitations can be made more meaningful as in-service activities for educators. May be rented for $7.00 or purchased for $75.00.

INDEX

I

Identifying major concepts, 67
Implementation, 125, 126, 130
Independent study, 131
Individual differences, 35–36
Individual differentiation, 107
Individual, worth of, 33–34
Individualized instruction, 6, 25, 26, 36, 42,
    84, 124, 130, 133, 150
Individualized learning, 137
Informal leadership, 74
Inquiry, 42
Interaction, student, 25
Interaction, students and teachers, 43

L

LAPs, 68–70, 110–111, 130, 131
Learning, 104
Learning Activities Packages, 6, 68–70,
    110
Learning, freedom in, 36
Learning, student responsibility in, 37
Learning, teacher-directed, 39
Level, 80, 124

M

Major learning concept, 81
Methods, 111
Model schools project, 130, 132, 133, 152,
    160
Modular scheduling, 6
Motivation, extrinsic, 106
Motivation, intrinsic, 106

N

Nongraded, 6, 24
Norm-referenced measurement, 116, 118

O

Objections to objectives, 90
Objective, 124
Open classrooms, 6, 25, 133
Open school, 109

P

Parent-centered curriculum, 45–46
Perceived purpose, 106
Philosophy, 32–33
Post-test, 83
Preassessment, 81, 105, 106, 109, 116
Prescription, 97, 106, 109
Pretest, 81, 105, 111
Principal, as facilitator of change, 66, 73
Process-oriented teaching, 40, 96
Process versus product, 179
Product-oriented teaching, 40–41, 96
Programmed learning, 112

R

Recording, 124
Reporting pupil progress, 189
Reporting system, 119, 124

S

Scope, 80
Self-testing, 82
Sequence, 80
Staff involvement, 65
Structure, 79, 124, 132, 133, 173
Students as self-actualizers, 38, 43
Subject-centered curriculum, 45, 46

T

Taxonomy of Educational Objectives, 95
Teacher-advisor, 132
Teacher, as consultant and advisor, 39–40
Teacher, as diagnostician, 42
Teacher-made tests, 80
Team teaching, 7
Test-item objectives, 31, 93
Time, 132
Tyler rationale, 45–46

U

Ungraded, 24

V

Visiting innovative schools, 66
Voucher system, 4, 6, 7